SHARKPEDIA

DK Publishing

LONDON, NEW YORK, MUNICH,
MELBOURNE, AND DELHI

Editor NANCY ELLWOOD

Writers NANCY ELLWOOD and MARGARET PARRISH

Designer JESSICA PARK

Managing Art Editor MICHELLE BAXTER

Publishing Director BETH SUTINIS

Art Director DIRK KAUFMAN

Production Manager IVOR PARKER

DTP Coordinator KATHY FARIAS

Picture Researcher CHRISSY MCINTYRE

First Edition, 2008

12 13 14 15 10 9 8 7 6 5 4 3 2 1

007-SD368-06/08

Published in the United States

by DK Publishing
375 Hudson Street, New York, New York 10014

Published in Great Britain by Dorling Kindersley Limited.

DK books are available at special discounts for bulk purchases
for sales promotions, premiums, fund-raising, or educational use.
For details, contact:

DK Publishing Special Markets
375 Hudson Street, New York, NY 10014
SpecialSales@dk.com

A complete catalog record for this title is available
from the Library of Congress

ISBN 978-0-7566-3761-3

Color reproduction by Colourscan, Singapore

Printed and bound in China by Leo

Discover more at www.dk.com

Contents

All Aboard the Lucky Chum

Calling all shark trackers! I'm Professor John Bigelow Finnegan, marine biologist and dedicated shark tracker. The name's a mouthful, I know, which is why my chums call me Big Finn. You can call me that, too, if you're fish enough to join me on my latest shark safari: a 'round-the-globe expedition to study these mighty and mysterious creatures.

We'll hit favorite shark haunts and hideouts, and study lots of different sharks—from the shy and the small to the gentle and the giant, and, of course, those celebrities of the sea, the mako, hammerhead, tiger, and great white.

But before we get going, listen up and learn the rules of the road—well, in this case, water—that are listed below.

TRAVEL TIPS BEFORE YOU SET SAIL

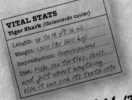

VITAL STATS
Tiger Shark (Galeocerdo cuvier)
Length: up to 18 ft (6 m)
Weight: 1,300 lbs (600 kg)
Reproduction: ovoviviparous
Diet: fish, sea turtles, seals, and just about anything else it can sink its teeth into

MAPPED OUT
Check out the maps to see where sharks roam. Some maps feature more than one shark. In those cases, the colors on the map correspond to the color of the shark's common name on the same page. (i.e., swell shark is highlighted in blue, so it will be shown in blue on the map.)

MAKING AN ID
Vitals Stats boxes at the start of each section provide a quick rundown of the special characteristics of the species we're studying.

CONSERVATION ALERT!
Note these alarm stickers telling us which sharks are in danger of becoming extinct and which are in the clear.

FISH BAIT
These bones will lead you to the belly of the beast—literally. Find out here what (or whom?!) the sharks like to eat.

SEAWORTHY SCIENCE
We'll be taking this journey on the *Lucky Chum*, which is chock-full of the latest equipment that serious trackers and scientists use. Take a look around and familiarize yourself with the tools of the trade.

STUDY AT SEA

- **Feeling cagey:** Swimming with sharks can be dangerous, so photographers and marine biologists who want to get near large predators like the great white often do so from the safety of a large metal cage. Wise choice.

- **In shining armor:** When up close and personal with smaller, less aggressive sharks, a chain-mail suit can protect against bites. This is old technology made new—chain mail was first worn by medieval knights to deflect sword slashes.

- **Taking the bait:** To study sharks, you've first got to find them. Enter chum, a "tasty" mixture of ground-up fish, blood, and oil. It's tossed into the water, and sharks find it irresistible. Not all scientists use chum. Some use decoys or other kinds of bait.

Sonic tag

- **You're it!:** Sharks are constantly on the move in the wild, often diving deeper than people can go, which makes it tough to keep track of them. To follow sharks, scientists attach sonic tags to their fins. This is done with great care, so the animals aren't harmed. Radio receivers pick up the signals from the tags so the animals can be tracked, and if a shark is caught, the catcher knows whom to contact so vital info doesn't go to waste.

- **"Say Chum!":** Underwater cameras make it possible for filmmakers and photographers to capture images of these fantastic creatures.

- **Logging it:** Science is about observation and study; computers make for very handy logbooks where data can be recorded and analyzed.

- **Scuba gear:** In the oceans, it's man who is the fish out of water. With scuba gear, however, we can level the playing field. Short for self-contained underwater breathing apparatus, modern scuba came into being in 1943, when Jacques-Yves Cousteau and Émile Gagnan invented the regulator (which allows you to control the flow of air from a tank while underwater). But people had learned to use hollow reeds as snorkels way back in the year 300. Around 1300, the Persians added rudimentary goggles to the mix. The equipment has improved a bit since then.

- **Safety first:** Cuts, scrapes, and nicks come with the shark-tracking territory, which is why it's always necessary to play it safe and have a fully stocked first aid kit on board.

A wet suit keeps you warm.

Flippers help you keep up with the fish.

I hope it's waterproof.

You can never have too many bandages.

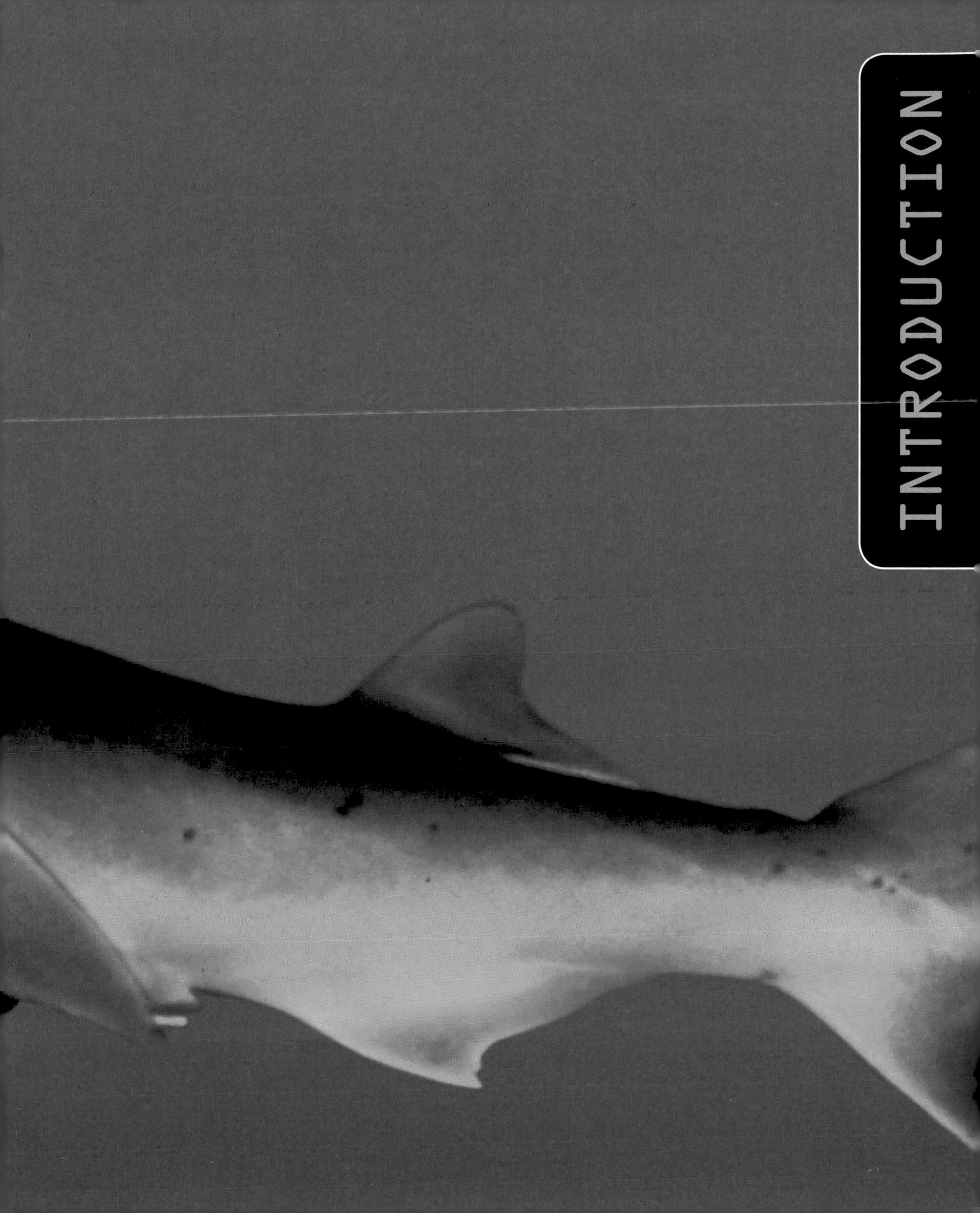

FEAR AND FOLKLORE

The fierce and fascinating shark looms large in sea folklore. Since people first hit open water, they have swapped stories about giant, man-eating sea monsters—from the ancient Leviathan, which swallowed ships whole, to the deadly Kraken of Viking lore, to sea serpents that looked more like dragons than fish.

And, of course, one of the oldest stories of the sea is the Old Testament tale of Jonah and the whale. In an ongoing biblical whodunit, experts still debate whether the "great fish" that swallowed Jonah was, in fact, a great white shark and not a whale.

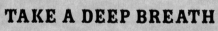

Hawaiian shark hook

LOOSE LIPS ... MAKE FOR A VERY BAD CATCH

Long ago, on the island of Hawaii, there lived a beautiful girl named Kalei. While swimming, Kalei caught the eye of Ka-moho-alii, king of the sharks. Lucky for him, he could shape-shift, and so took the form of a man. Together, they had a son, Nanaue, who was born with a strange deformity on his back: the gaping mouth of a shark.

Eventually, the shark king returned to the sea and Kalei raised her son alone. She tried to tame his true nature, but as he grew as a man, he also grew as a shark. At the shore, he would ask fishermen where they were headed, and then, after morphing into a shark, would pick off the best of their catch, leaving the people hungry. When the villagers figured out what was happening, they decided to make shark bait of Nanaue. To escape, Nanaue turned into a shark and went to live with Dad at sea. Since then, fishermen never tell anyone where they fish. Lesson learned.

In 1815, while sailing aboard the *Bellerophon*, a defeated Napoleon was lured from his stately cabin to see a shark that had been pulled aboard.

TAKE A DEEP BREATH

Part shark, part octopus, Lusca is a legendary creature "native" to the Bahamas. She guards the dark blue holes that are home to conches, lobsters, grouper, and sharks. Legend has it that her breath controls the tidal currents that bring these inhabitants their food.

BITING BACK

Superstition and the sea go hand in hand. In the South Pacific, some locals believe that the tooth of a man-eating shark brings protection and a long, prosperous life, which explains why many divers won't hit the water without a toothy talisman.

The story goes that Ohav-Lai, god of the seas, was challenged by a shark for supremacy of the seas. After days of battle, Ohav-Lai emerged victorious, with a shark tooth hanging from his neck. And so it has been ever since . . .

FOLKLORE IN A FLASH

- Ancient Polynesians often believed that sharks were spirits sent by sorcerers to bring bad luck.
- In the Solomon Islands, hunters carried carvings that had a shark on one side and a bonito fish on the other in the hope that these charms would repel sharks and attract fish.
- Solomon Islanders believed that when people died their ghosts entered the bodies of sharks. The Solomon sea spirit has a man's head and shark fins.
- In Borneo, the saw of a sawfish is hung over babies' cradles to keep them from crying. (Maybe it helps them cut their teeth?)
- In Fiji, the half man–half shark Dakuwaqa has protected the island and its fishermen ever since losing a battle with an octopus!

A REAL FISHY TALE: THE CASE OF THE SHARK PAPERS

Honesty really is the best policy. That's the moral of this story, and something that American Thomas Briggs, captain of the *Nancy*, ended up learning the hard way. What follows may sound like a big fish tale, but it's more like a case of truth being stranger than fiction.

The date is July 3, 1799, and the *Nancy* sets sail from Baltimore, Maryland, headed for the Dutch West Indian island of Curacao. On the homeward leg of the trip the plan is to swing by Haiti and pick up coffee. At first, things go swimmingly, but then bad weather hits and Captain Briggs has to put in at Aruba, where he takes the opportunity to load up on stolen loot. To cover his tracks, Briggs forges a logbook and throws the real one into the sea. He then sets sail for Haiti, but never makes it there.

On August 28, Commander Hugh Whylie of the British cutter the *Sparrow* captures the *Nancy*.

He's certain the captain isn't on the up-and-up and that the ship is carrying stolen goods, which under British law belong to the crown. Whylie files a lawsuit in Kingston, Jamaica, and Briggs promptly countersues. At first, it looks like Briggs will get off scot-free, until fickle fate—and the voracious appetite of a shark—intervene.

While breakfasting with his friend Lieutenant Michael Fitton on board the HMS *Abergavenny*, Commander Whylie learns that a strange object has been found in the belly of a shark caught by the crew. That object is none other than the original *Nancy* logbook, which, when presented in court, proves that Briggs has indeed cooked the books. Thanks to the Shark Papers, as they came to be known, Briggs is convicted.

If you go to the Institute of Jamaica in Kingston today you can see the Shark Papers, along with the jaws of the actual shark that ate them. Although the jaws are now housed at the Institute, for a time they hung over the courthouse as a reminder that honesty is the best policy.

PREHISTORIC SHARKS
WHAT A LONG, STRANGE TRIP IT'S BEEN

To say that sharks have staying power is putting it mildly. Sharks were prowling the oceans long before the dinosaurs made it to the party. The oldest shark fossils—found in Australia and Antarctica—date back more than 400 million years.

The design of the shark must have been pretty good from the get-go, because it has held up over time. Like their modern descendents, ancient sharks had gills, sandpaper-like skin, and skeletons of cartilage. (Cartilage is the rubbery stuff that gives your ears and nose shape.) And, like today's sharks, these long-ago predators were probably carnivores.

Ichthyosaurus

TIME TRAVEL

Back in the day (the late Ordovician Period), the seas were teeming with fish and invertebrates such as squid and mollusks. By the Mesozoic Era, it was the age of reptiles, and dinosaurs ruled the land. Come the Cenozoic Era, birds and mammals became king of the hill.

PALEOZIOC ERA 543–250 mya (million years ago)

	Cambrian Period 543–490 mya	Ordovician Period 490–443 mya	Silurian Period 443–417 mya	Devonian Period 417–354 mya	Carboniferous Period 354–290 mya	Permian Period 290–250 mya
Landlubbers	Pretty quiet. No signs of animal life; lichens and fungi are the only plants.		Insects make their first appearance.	Some intrepid fish leave the waters, giving rise to amphibians.	Dragonflies and those modern-city scourges—cockroaches—enter the scene, together with reptiles. From reptiles come the first archosaurs, the ruling reptiles.	
Seafarers	The first vertebrates (backboned animals) lived in the oceans. They were called agnatha, "fish without jaws."	Some fish get jaws, and the world welcomes a new group of fish called chondrichthyans, which were the forebears of sharks, rays, skates, and chimaeras.		*Stethacanthus* and *Xenacanthus* were here.		

MESOZOIC ERA 250–65 mya

	Triassic Period 250–206 mya	Jurassic Period 206–144 mya	Cretaceous Period 144–65 mya
Land-lubbers	The Age of Dinos begins. *Eoraptor* is the earliest dinosaur. First flying reptiles appear.	*Stegosaurus* thrives. Some dinos evolve into birds.	Birds and large dinos rule. It's *T. rex*'s last stand.
Seafarers	Reptiles adapt to the oceans: Their limbs become paddles. If you had gone scuba diving then, you would have run across long-necked plesiosaurs, dolphinlike ichthyosaurs, and the archaic shark, *Hybodus*.		

BIG BOYS (AND GIRLS)

The great white (or white shark) may be king of the modern aquatic beasts, but it is a small fry compared to *Carcharodon megalodon*. It's hard to tell from fossil records just what *C. megalodon* looked like, but paleobiologists estimate that this mega-monster weighed 50 tons (45 metric tons), measured 50 feet (15 m), and had 6-inch (15-cm) teeth. Its jaws were so big that a grown man could have stood inside. Top marine seadog for 14 million years, *C. megalodon* died out two million years ago.

DENTAL RECORDS

Sharks have left behind lots of fossilized evidence of where and when they lived, mostly in the form of teeth, spines, and denticles. (The sharks' cartilage skeletons usually rot away before they can form fossils.)

The white shark's tooth is dwarfed by . . .

. . . *C. megalodon*'s massive tooth.

C. megalodon

white shark

TOOTHY GRIN

The biggest shark teeth ever found belonged to *C. megalodon*; they dwarf the white shark's choppers.

CENOZOIC ERA 65 mya–today

	Paleogene Period 65–23 mya	Neogene Period 23 mya–today
Landlubbers	Big upheaval! A catastrophic event leads to the extinction of many species, including dinosaurs. Hominids (our anscestors) show up. So do birds, frogs, lizards, and snakes.	The hominid *Australopithecus* lived two mya; *Homo sapiens* were in Africa 150,000 years ago; the Ice Age finished 20,000 year ago. And here we are today!
Seafarers	In swims an enormous shark, *Carcharodon megalodon*, or "huge tooth."	Familiar territory: modern sharks, plus too many magnificent sea creatures to list.

IT'S A FAMILY AFFAIR

Sharks have a large group of cartilaginous cousins: the rays, or batoids (including sawfish, skates, and guitarfish), and chimaeras, or holocephalans. All have rubbery cartilage skeletons and gill slits like their shark kinfolk. They also lack a swim bladder, and rely on a large, buoyant liver.

Batoid traits are clear: Guitarfish, rays, and skates look a lot like flattened angel sharks, which isn't surprising, since rays evolved from sharks 200 million years ago. Members of this branch of the family tree are usually harmless, although some rays can give a nasty sting with their tails.

SOCIAL SCENE

Many rays like a good get-together: Mantas may congregate in patches of food-rich water, and cownose rays dine in schools.

At mating time, rays group together, with most batoids giving birth to a few pups. Skates, however, lay several cased eggs, which they anchor to the seabed with horns or tendrils.

SHOCKING NEWS

Electric rays give predators and prey a jolt by stunning them with electric shocks. This is bad news for divers, who may inadvertently find themselves zapped.

RAY'S ANATOMY

- All rays have winglike pectoral fins that run the length of their bodies.
- A ray's mouth and gill slits are on the underside of its body. To breathe while lying on the seafloor, a ray can draw water in through a pair of openings on its head, called spiracles.
- Rays are partial to worms, crustaceans, and mollusks. Their teeth can crush shellfish armor, allowing them to get to the tasty morsels inside.
- Many of these bottom-dwellers have eyes on the tops of their heads, the better to see predators swimming above.
- A pale underside and mottled topside make for good camouflage for many batoids.
- Like sharks, rays have ampullae of Lorenzini—organs that can sense electric signals from other animals. Think of it as "ray-dar"!

Guitarfish

Sawfish

Did you know? There are more than 600 different types of ray found around the world, both in oceans and freshwater, and in warm and cool temperatures.

Enormous manta ray

A DEVIL OF A FISH

Manta rays, or devilfish, are huge. Their enormous wings measure up to 23 feet (7 m)—as wide as four cars! Like the biggest sharks, these "devils" are harmless filter-feeders that channel plankton into their wide mouths. This female manta, caught off the coast of New Jersey, weighed nearly 2,900 lbs (1,315 kg).

POETRY IN MOTION

Rays glide gracefully through the water by beating their wings in slow, rhythmic motions. This movement is particularly pronounced in the large species, such as the mighty manta. But don't mistake ease of motion for lack of power—big rays can leap out of the water, sometimes as high as 5 feet (1.5 m).

DEEP-SEA DOPPELGÄNGERS?

Thornback ray

- Often mistaken for each other, the sawfish and sawshark are near look-alikes. But unlike sawsharks, sawfish don't have barbels on their saws and their gill slits are on their undersides, not their heads. Both species use their saws for feeding and for putting up a fight.
- Thornback ray is often sold as edible common skate, but it's not the real deal. Skate is about twice as big, growing up to 7 feet (2 m).

WHAT'S IN A NAME?

- Stingrays come by their name honestly: Venomous barbs on their tails deliver quite a sting.
- Some species, such as the starry ray and thornback ray, are armed with prickly spines along their backs.
- Chimaeras—or ratfish, as they're often called—get their nickname from their ratlike tails. Living in the ocean depths, the ratfish has beaklike teeth and a hook on its head resembling the one sported by the ancient *Hybodus*.
- River rays live, not surprisingly, in freshwater.
- A sharklike ray, the guitarfish lives in warmer waters and looks like the musical instrument, with a round body and broad-ish tail.
- One particularly strange-looking chimaera is called the elephant fish. You guessed it—its snout is shaped like an elephant's trunk.
- Sailors called the gentle manta by the misnomer "devilfish," after the "horns" that stick out from its head.

Stingray

Let's get acquainted...

Whoa! There's a lot of info here. But we've got to learn about these animals from the inside out, so let's get to it! What is a shark anyway? All sharks are predatory fish belonging to the group chondrichthyes (fish whose skeletons are made from cartilage, not bone). There are more than four hundred species of shark worldwide, and while they're all different, they tend to follow the same plan as this guy below.

Did you know?
Cartilage doesn't contain any blood vessels like bone does.

Dorsal fin keeps the shark upright.

SHE'S YAR, MATEY!
The tail is the shark's propeller, powering it forward. Tail shape makes a big difference when it comes to speed—sharks with equal-sized tail lobes, like the mako, are swifties, while the slowpokes, such as the swell shark, may have hardly any lower lobe at all.

Tail fin sweeps side to side to propel the shark forward.

HOT AND COLD
Most sharks are cold-bodied, and when your muscles are cold, they move more slowly. But the faster sharks have an amazing adaptation: They are warm-bodied. This means their muscles are always warm and ready to pounce should lunch dart by.

WE LIKE LIVER
• Sharks have a large, two-lobed liver that has two main functions: It helps in digestion and it keeps the shark afloat. Unlike bony fishes that have an air-filled swim bladder, sharks rely on the oil in their livers to keep them from sinking.
• Shark liver is full of a chemical called squalene, which is lighter (or less dense) than water. Squalene is useful in keeping the shark afloat, but it can also be used as an antibiotic.

Did you know?
All newborn sharks are left to fend for themselves immediately after birth.

HEARTWARMING
A shark's heart lies close to the gills, much like a human heart lies close to the lungs. That way, blood that has just taken up oxygen can be pumped to the rest of the shark's body, and blood loaded with carbon dioxide can make its way back to the gills to stock up on fresh oxygen. Ta-da! Shark respiration!

FLESH AND . . . CARTILAGE
Shark skeletons are made of a gristly material called cartilage. Cartilage is tough and flexible, but it's not hard like bone is. To help support the hard work these hunters do, the cartilage in the back, jaw, and brain case of a shark is hardened with minerals, including calcium.

NUTRITION FIRST

After it takes that initial bite, a shark's meal passes through its gullet and into its stomach, where digestion begins. Food goes to the intestine, which contains a multilayered scroll valve that increases the area that absorbs digested food. The gallbladder releases a fluid to help in fat absorption, while the liver does its bit to break down fats, carbohydrates, and proteins.

Diet plan
sharks can go for surprisingly long periods without eating: Great whites can manage for months without a meal.

UNDERWATER BREATHING APPARATUS

All sharks have gills—either five, six, or seven of them on each side—that lie behind the head. The shark "inhales" by taking water into its mouth and keeping the gill slits closed. To "exhale," the shark opens the gill slits and pushes the water out. As the water rushes over the gills, oxygen is absorbed and carbon dioxide is released.

SMART COOKIE

The ratio of brain to brawn in sharks is higher than in most bony fish, and equals that of some mammals.

BIG SNIFFER

The olfactory bulb takes up lots of room in the brain, which shows how keen the sense of smell is in a shark.

Liver

Heart

Pectoral fins steady the shark and provide lift.

GETTING A GRIP

Sharks have upper and lower jaws that are only loosely attached to their skulls. This allows top-notch predators like the white shark to push their jaws forward to nab prey.

PEARLY WHITES

When a tooth falls out, a spare moves in from behind. A shark may grow as many as 30 thousand new teeth in its lifetime.

MAKING BABIES

Though scientists know very little about shark mating, they do know this: All male sharks have a pair of claspers near their pelvic fins. During mating, sperm travels down a clasper and into an opening on the female's body called the cloaca, where it fertilizes the eggs in the oviducts.

BABY SHARKS ARE BORN IN ONE OF THREE WAYS:

- Viviparous (or placental viviparous) sharks give birth to live young, as humans do. The shark develops inside the mother's body and is attached to her by an umbilical cord. Baby sharks are born fully formed and able to fend for themselves.
- Oviparous sharks deposit eggs on the seafloor after they've been fertilized inside the female's body. Egg shape and size vary greatly, but all have a way to anchor themselves to rocks, reefs, grasses, or whatever's nearby.
- Ovoviviparous (or aplacental viviparous) sharks rely on a dual approach. These sharks carry their fertilized eggs inside their bodies. The developing pups are nourished by a yolk sac instead of a placenta. Some species also dine on unfertilized eggs inside the womb, a practice called oophagy. And some species take it to another level and eat their smaller siblings in the uterus! Once ready, the baby sharks swim out into the great blue yonder.

ALL CREATURES GREAT AND SMALL

The size of sharks varies widely: from the tiny dwarf dogshark at 6 inches (15 cm) to the giant whale shark of 40 feet (12 m). Most sharks average around 3 feet (1 m).

ON THE OUTSIDE

Sharks don't have scales like bony fish. Their bodies are covered with small, hard "skin teeth" called dermal denticles. These structures are raised and often have ridges. They're usually tightly packed next to one another and help keep the shark's body streamlined.

IT'S ALL IN ORDER

Sharks are grouped into eight orders. While they're all cartilaginous fish, sometimes that's all they have in common. Check out the chart below.

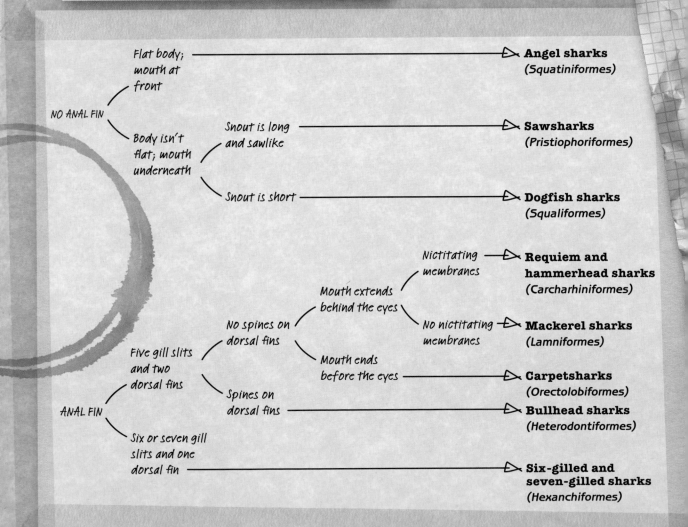

NO ANAL FIN

Flat body; mouth at front — **Angel sharks** *(Squatiniformes)*

Body isn't flat; mouth underneath

Snout is long and sawlike — **Sawsharks** *(Pristiophoriformes)*

Snout is short — **Dogfish sharks** *(Squaliformes)*

ANAL FIN

Five gill slits and two dorsal fins

No spines on dorsal fins

Mouth extends behind the eyes

Nictitating membranes — **Requiem and hammerhead sharks** *(Carcharhiniformes)*

No nictitating membranes — **Mackerel sharks** *(Lamniformes)*

Mouth ends before the eyes — **Carpetsharks** *(Orectolobiformes)*

Spines on dorsal fins — **Bullhead sharks** *(Heterodontiformes)*

Six or seven gill slits and one dorsal fin — **Six-gilled and seven-gilled sharks** *(Hexanchiformes)*

sense-itive souls

Now that we've been inside and out of a shark's anatomy, let's take a closer look at its senses. I mean, you can't be the king of the sea without having an edge, right? A shark's super-sharp senses come in handy for finding a meal, keeping out of harm's way, navigating the seas, and meeting a mate.

EYE SPY

Sharks have exceptional eyesight. Their eyes usually sit on either side of their heads, but not always. Bottom-dwellers, such as the wobbegong, often have eyes on the tops of their heads. And hammerheads' eyes are on the ends of their wide, T-shaped heads, which they swing from side to side to take in the scenery.

epaulette shark's eye

catshark's eye

THE BETTER TO SEE YOU WITH, MY DEAR!

- Sharks have great night vision and see 10 times better than we do in dim light. This is thanks to a mirrorlike layer at the back of the eye called the tapetum lucidum; if you were to shine a light in their eyes, they'd glow green or yellow like a cat's.
- A shark's pupils get bigger or smaller depending on how bright it is—a feature that's common in mammals, but rare in fish.
- Like a human retina, a shark retina contains rods and cones; rods are sensitive to light changes and cones probably allow the shark to see their world in color.

LINE DRIVE

All sharks have a row of tiny receptor cells, called neuromasts, running down their sides and around their heads. This is called the lateral line. These sensors detect the movement and position of prey and whether it's thrashing around, which is a good thing from the shark's point of view. After all, injured prey makes for easy pickings. Strangely enough, neuromast receptors can be shut down while the shark is putting on the feedbag.

horn shark's eye

THE BARBEL OF SEA-VILLE

Some sharks, such as the nurse shark, have feelers—called barbels—on the ends of their noses. Barbels are useful for poking around in the sand and seabed when looking for food, and may also aid in smelling and tasting.

Ornate wobbegong with barbels

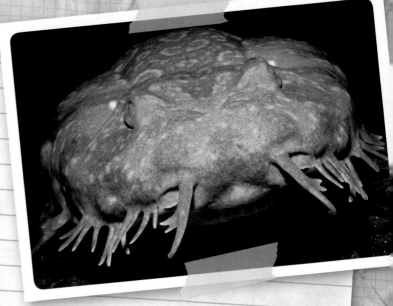

SPIT TEST

Considering that sharks have a bad rep for being insatiable eating machines, it may come as a surprise to know that taste is their least-developed sense. Taste buds in the mouth and throat (though not on the tongue) help sharks figure out if a meal is yummy or yucky. Not known for having refined manners, sharks may bite prey to see if it's tasty; if it's not, out it goes. Potential prey use all kinds of devices to keep themselves off the menu. Finless sole, for instance, are covered in a nasty-tasting slime that makes them a culinary no-go.

The nose knows

Sharks' nostrils are used only for smelling (not breathing). Seawater flows over the nostrils, bringing chemical clues as to what's nearby.

BLOOD IN THE WATER

Sharks have such a keen sense of smell that they can detect tiny amounts of blood from more than a mile (1.6 km) away. And I mean tiny: These super smellers can detect blood that has been diluted more than a million times. They can sniff out other things, too. The blacktip reef shark can smell just one drop of fish extract mixed into the equivalent of an Olympic-sized swimming pool. And the hungrier the animal gets, the sharper its sense of smell.

DID YOU KNOW?

- Canals in the inner ear help the shark orient itself in the water in much the same way as our ears help us balance.
- To a shark, vibrations of water molecules are heard as sound.
- Sharks are best at hearing low-frequency sounds—much better than we are.
- Sharks can hear noises from over 700 feet (213 m) away.

NOW 'EAR THIS!

Sharks have ears, but you can't see them: They're inside the head. The ears consist of three semicircular canals that resemble those in the ears of other vertebrates. Receptors in the inner ear pick up sounds traveling through the water. Each ear has a duct leading to a pore on the shark's head, which is the path the sound waves take on their way to the brain.

IT'S ELECTRIFYING!

Sharks go us one better in the sensory stakes: They literally have a sixth sense, called electroreception. This electrosense allows sharks to detect the subtle electrical fields sent out by other animals.

Electroreception is probably the most intriguing animal sense, and the rarest. Only sharks and the duck-billed platypus of Australia are thought to have this sense. Here's how it works:

All organisms emit electrical signals. Sharks have organs, called the ampullae of Lorenzini, that can pinpoint the strength and location of an electric field—even if it's coming from an animal hiding motionless in the seabed. The ampullae are delicate, jelly-filled canals connected to pores in the shark's skin and located around the snout. These babies are so sensitive they can detect electrical fields of one hundred-millionth of a volt.

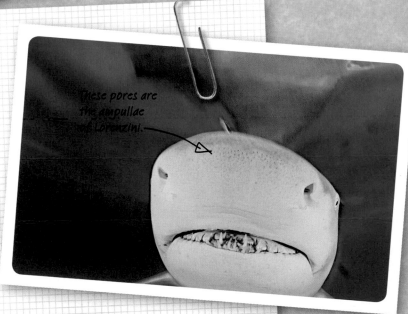

These pores are the ampullae of Lorenzini.

MAGNETIC ATTRACTION

Sharks make the rounds of the seas, and seem to know where they're going. It's thought that the ampullae of Lorenzini also act as a built-in compass, tuning sharks in to the Earth's magnetic field and helping them navigate the waters.

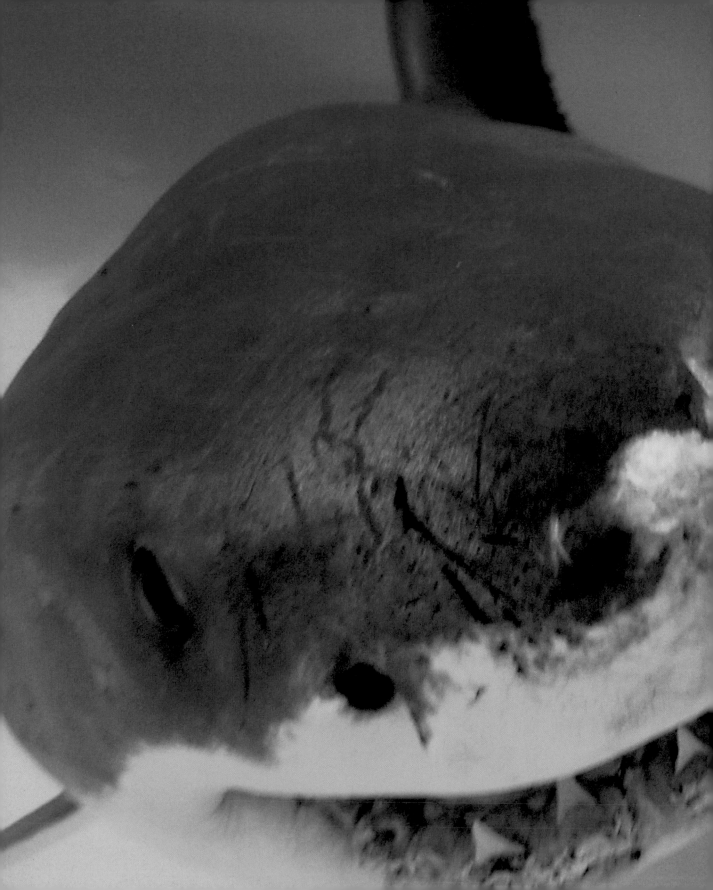

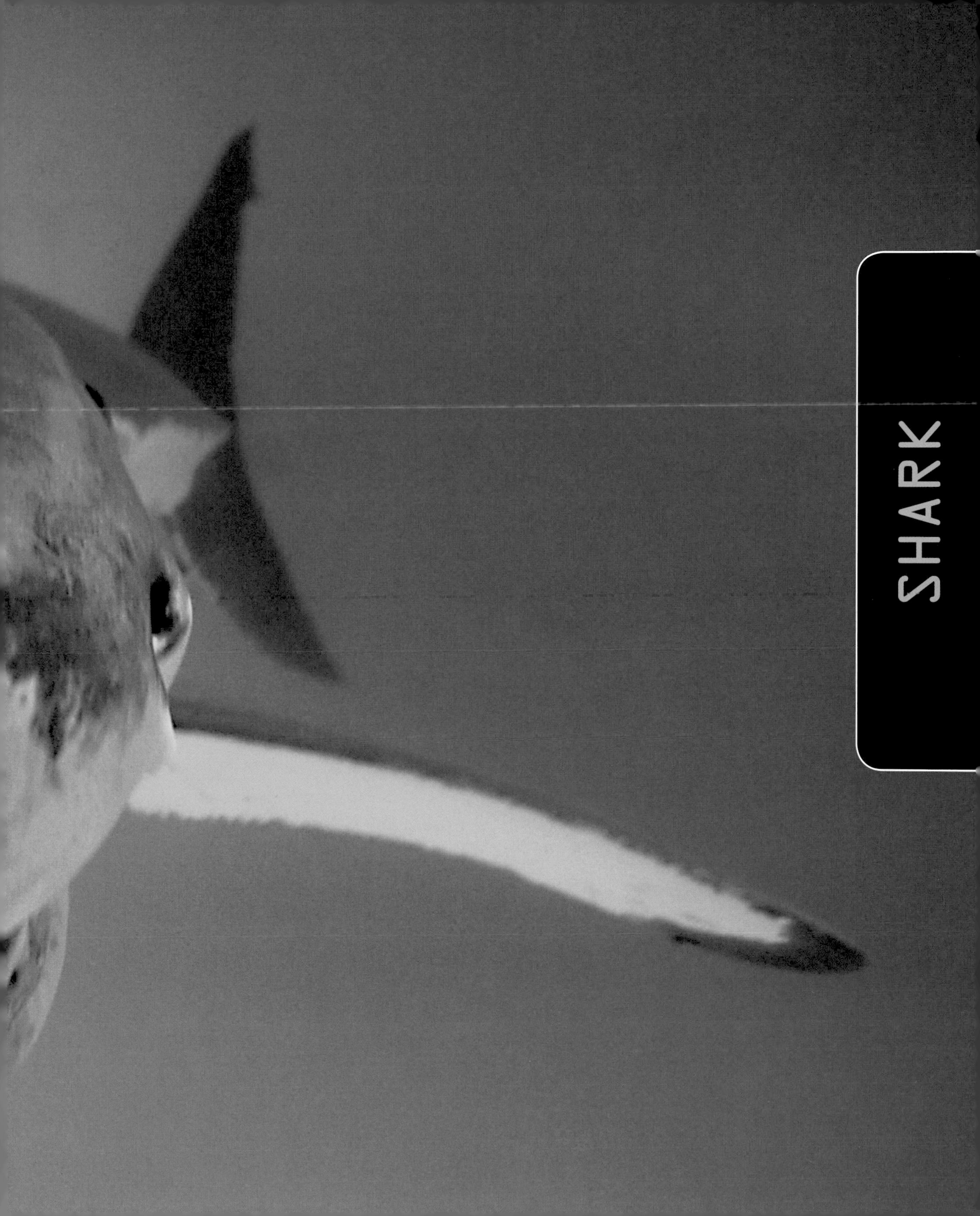

SHARK

SEA DOGS

Okay, so you've got your sea legs and we're ready to go. Let's start small and docile, shall we? We'll first visit the dogs of the sea, from the order Squaliformes (dogfish sharks).

PYGMY SHARK

The pygmy shark *(Euprotomicrus bispinatus)* is one of the smallest shark species in the world, with females topping out at about 11 inches (28 cm) (the males are smaller).

HOW LOW CAN YOU GO?

Like many shark species, the pygmy shark practices vertical migration. This is when the shark spends its night hunting near the surface, but its days way down deep. The pygmy shark has been recorded deeper than 5,000 feet (1,524 m).

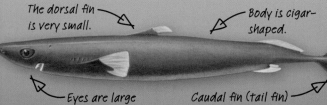

The dorsal fin is very small.

Body is cigar-shaped.

Eyes are large and round.

Caudal fin (tail fin) is paddle-shaped.

GLOWING REVIEWS

The pygmy shark has a luminescent belly that glows gently. This probably attracts prey and mates.

SLIMY LIGHTS

This dogfish shark is part of the genus *Etmopterus*, or the lantern sharks. All the sharks in this group produce slimy mucus that glows in the dark. The slime is probably a deterrent to predators, while the ability to glow in deep water probably attracts prey to this unique fish.

VELVET BELLY

Named for its dark (often black) belly, *Etmopterus spinax* is a stout lantern shark that lives in the eastern Atlantic Ocean. It grows to lengths of about 16 inches (40 cm), and eats squid and crustaceans.

Front dorsal fin is smaller than the rear dorsal fin.

In front of each dorsal fin is a spike.

PIKED DOGFISH

Perhaps the world's most abundant shark is the piked— or spiny—dogfish *(Squalus acanthias),* found around the world in cool, temperate waters. Because of their incredible numbers, these sharks are fished commercially for food. Their liver and skin are also of value: the liver for its oil, and the skin to be sold as leather. As a result, populations of piked dogfish in the North Atlantic have plummeted due to overfishing.

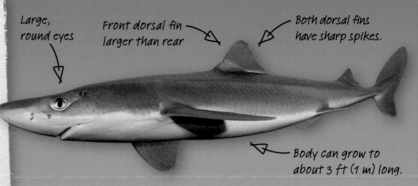

Large, round eyes

Front dorsal fin larger than rear

Both dorsal fins have sharp spikes.

Body can grow to about 3 ft (1 m) long.

SHARK ANYONE?

Piked dogfish like to feast on small fish, squid, and crustaceans. Sometimes they'll even snack on piked dogfish pups. Because of this cannibalistic tendency, pregnant females usually stick to the coasts where their newly born pups can get out of harm's way fast.

The large dorsal fins are wide and sail-shaped.

Each dorsal fin has two spikes.

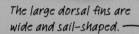

PRICKLY DOGFISH

There's a group of dogfish called rough sharks that differ in appearance from their dogfish cousins. The prickly dogfish *(Oxynotus bruniensis)* is probably one of the most distinct.

ROUGH RIDERS

This family of sharks gets its name from the particularly rough skin that covers its stout, humpbacked body. The prickly dogfish sports large, sail-shaped dorsal fins—the first of which is much larger than the second.

VITAL STATS
Dogfish Sharks (Order Squaliformes)

Length: usually no greater than 4 ft (1.2 m)

Reproduction: some species are oviparous, while others are ovoviviparous

Diet: crustaceans, mollusks, squid, small fish

Conservation status: many species are vulnerable or threatened due to overfishing and slow reproduction rates

CATNIP

As we continue our visit with the smaller, docile sharks of the world, we come upon the feline-monikered catsharks. As a group, these fabulous sharks are distinguished by their streamlined bodies, catlike eyes, and small dorsal fins that are set far back on their bodies.

WHERE IN THE WORLD?
Catsharks can be found around the world, mostly in tropical waters, often living near the seafloor.

PAJAMA CATSHARK

The pajama—or striped—catshark (*Poroderma africanum*) is one of the more distinctive catsharks due to its stripes. This pj-wearing shark also sports barbels on its snout, which it uses to sense crustaceans and small fish hidden in the seafloor.

> **Did you know?**
> This shark's stripes led to its name: They look like the stripes on the fabric traditionally used to make pajamas.

The dorsal fins are small and set far back.

Dark stripes run the length of the body.

Grows to be about 3 ft (1 m) long.

Anal fin

VITAL STATS
Catsharks (Family Scyliorhinidae)

Length: *usually no greater than 4 ft (1.2 m)*

Reproduction: *90 percent of species are oviparous, the remaining are ovoviviparous*

Diet: *crustaceans, mollusks, squid, small fish*

Conservation status: *many species are vulnerable or threatened due to overfishing and slow reproduction rates*

IS IT A DOGFISH OR A CATSHARK?

How to tell these elasmo-cousins apart? It's all in the fins:

DOGFISH:
- No anal fin
- First dorsal fin much larger than second
- First dorsal fin starts up near the pectoral fins

CATSHARK:
- Anal fin present
- Dorsal fins are close in size
- Dorsal fins set far back on the body, almost at the tail

CHAIN CATSHARK

Named for the chainlike pattern on its back, the chain catshark *(Scyliorhinus retifer)* lives along the eastern and Gulf coasts of North America, usually at depths from 500 to 1,000 feet (152 to 305 m). They live along the seabed and eat crustaceans, squid, and small fish.

Its unique coloration is one of the boldest among all species of shark.

The chain pattern is black or brown.

Denticles are narrow and flat, giving the skin a smooth texture.

NURSERY SCHOOL

Chains are oviparous, and scientists believe that females deposit their eggs in large groups called nurseries. If left undisturbed, these nurseries are often a safe place for the sharks to hatch. But if they're in the line of a bottom trawling boat, an entire generation of catsharks can be wiped out in one fell swoop.

SWELL SHARK

Another famous catshark is the swell shark *(Cephaloscyllium ventriosum)*. Swell sharks grow to be up to 4 feet (1.2 m) long, and live only in the eastern Pacific Ocean. They're known for their ability to fill up with air or water when they're threatened, which swells their bodies.

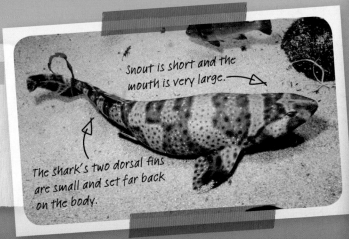

Snout is short and the mouth is very large.

The shark's two dorsal fins are small and set far back on the body.

If brought to the surface, a swell shark will also gulp air to perform its blow-up trick.

DRINK THIS

Swell sharks spend most of their day sitting in rocky outcroppings and kelp forests waiting for prey to come to them. If a hungry sea lion, seal, or larger shark swims by, the swell shark will gulp enough water to inflate its belly. This serves two purposes: 1. It makes the swell shark look larger, discouraging the predator, and 2. The fattened shark is now wedged in its rocky hiding spot and can't be pulled out. As soon as danger has swum by, the swell shark spits out the water and returns to normal size.

The Chondrichthyes Chronicles

"All the News That's Fit to Swim"

VOLUME I: EARLY EDITION

DATE: THURSDAY

PRICE: 50 CLAMS

SHARKY CURE FOR CANCER?

Can dogfish help humans?

By Dr. Ichthyo Pooch

People have thought for years that shark cartilage can prevent and/or cure cancer. That's not true. But scientists *have* recently discovered a shark-produced substance which can prevent tumor growth and act as an antibiotic.

It's called squalamine, and its found in the stomach and tissues of dogfish. Its most impressive trait is that it has angiogenic qualities. *Angiogenic* means that it stops tumors from creating the networks of blood vessels that they need to grow and invade other cells. This is an important discovery, as tumors are

Dogfish sharks are being studied around the world.

often very hard to stop. The antibiotic quality is quite exceptional, as it kills many different types of bacteria.

A century ago this kind of discovery could have been catastrophic for the world's dogfish populations (as every fortune-seeker out there would have tried to get in on the squalamine trade). But these days we have conservation in mind, and we approach squalamine research with an eye toward the health and well-being of these wonderful dogs of the sea.

GLOW-IN-THE-DARK SHARK?

By Swimm N. Shine

Deep in the sea there are creatures that have the fantastical ability to glow in the dark. Squid, fish, worms, crustaceans, and mollusks are all known to produce light, a phenomenon called bioluminescence. Along with these animals, there are

Since bottom-dwelling sharks are hard to study, little is known about them and their glowing talents. What we do know is that the sharks have cells on their bodies called photophores. These cells produce light, sometimes in conjunction with body-covering mucus.

Most researchers agree that the light draws in prey, and can attract mates. In fact, a lantern shark's light displays are species and gender specific, so mates can find one another in the darkness.

Closer to the surface, the photophores can mimic starlight and moonlight, which confuses predators looking up at the belly of their prey.

The cookiecutter shark's photophores glow green.

Whatever the reason for this special talent, this reporter is willing to bet that these sharks are the life of every holiday party.

many species of dogfish sharks that can light up the depths. In fact, this quality is exactly how the lantern sharks got their name.

MIDSIZED MAYHEM

Okay, tracker. You're doing great. Only a little seasick, but you're getting the hang of it. I think we can graduate to more intimidating-looking sharks. These are bigger, from a number of different families, but are all midsized and gorgeous. Let's see how you do. . . .

SHARPNOSE SEVENGILL SHARK

Heptranchias perlo is a bottom-dwelling shark that loves deep, temperate waters. It's often found at depths greater than 3,000 feet (almost 950 m).

Eyes are very large, and often green.

SHARK SAYS "MOO"?

The sharpnose sevengill is a member of the Hexanchidae family, or the cow sharks. The fish in this family sport six or seven gill slits, rather than the five that most sharks possess.

Snout is short and pointy.

SERIOUS APPETITE

Despite being a relatively small shark—females are larger than males and top out at about 4 feet (1.2 m)—the sharpnose sevengill is a voracious eater, especially in the evening hours. If you're having one over for dinner, be sure to stock up on plenty of shrimp, squid, lobsters, crabs, small bony fish, rays, skates, and other small sharks.

Single dorsal fin is small and set far back.

Seven gill slits decrease in size.

Elegant tail sports an elongated upper lobe.

BLUNTNOSE SIXGILL

And here's a six-gilled cousin in the cow shark family: the bluntnose sixgill shark *(Hexanchus griseus)*. Found in some of the same waters as the sharpnose sevengill, this much larger cow shark reaches lengths of more than 15 feet (4.6 m).

DEEP-SEA MYSTERY

Not much is known about the bluntnose sixgill, as it spends most of its life at extreme depths: down to 6,500 feet (1,981 m). It is considered a slow but strong swimmer and thought to be a solitary creature.

Tail has pronounced upper lobe (although not as elegant as the sevengill's).

As one might guess, there are six gill slits.

Lower jaw is populated with comb-like plates.

CROCODILE SHARK

Pseudocarcharias kamoharai is named for its tendency to snap its jaws like a crocodile when caught. A member of the mackerel family of sharks, the crocodile shark lives in the open ocean and dines on small bony fish, shrimp, and squid.

LIVER, ANYONE?

While the flesh of the crocodile shark isn't of much value, its squalene-rich liver is. These sharks are fished commercially in Japan.

Eyes are enormous (making this shark a good visual hunter).

Body is slender.

Gill slits are long, almost meeting at the top of the head.

COOKIECUTTER SHARK

While this little guy really isn't midsized, his impressive tooth action bumps him up into this group. I mean, he's actually named for the wounds he inflicts on prey, so I think he can play with the big boys.

SMALL BUT POWERFUL

Isistius brasiliensis is a small, cigar-shaped shark that tops out at about 20 inches (50 cm). It spends its days more than 3,200 feet (975 m) down, but comes up toward the surface at night to hunt. Its favorite meals? Large marine animals: tuna, sharks, dolphins, seals, and whales. It's even been known to damage submarines.

WHAT'S IN A NAME?

The cookiecutter attracts large animals with light-producing cells on its belly (called photophores). It bites the larger animal and holds fast with its lips and teeth, then spins its entire body, removing a circular chunk of flesh. What's left behind is a wound that looks like it was made by a cookie cutter.

This shark is ovoviviparous.

Lips act as suction cups while it is feeding.

The snout is short and cone-shaped.

The bottom teeth are triangular and interconnected. When they fall out, they do so as one unit (think dentures!).

LEOPARD SHARK

Named for its lovely pattern of large and small spots, the leopard shark *(Triakis semifasciata)* lives in the eastern Pacific Ocean, along the North American coast from Oregon down to Mexico.

SOCIAL SWIMMER

Unlike many other types of shark, the leopard forms large schools, sometimes including other species such as smoothhounds and spiny dogfish.

Dorsal fins are close in size.

Snout is broad and rounded.

Body grows to about 6 ft (1.8 m) and is covered in spots.

TOPE SHARK

The tope shark *(Galeorhinus galeus)* is a member of the Triakidae family (aka the houndsharks) and is rather common, found in temperate waters around the world. Despite the name "houndshark," the tope shark is actually a type of catshark.

A SHARK BY ANY OTHER NAME . . .

The tope is also called the soupfin shark, as its fins are a favorite in the shark fin soup market.

Body is long and lean. Females grow up to 6 ft (1.8 m); males are a little smaller.

Eyes are large and almond-shaped.

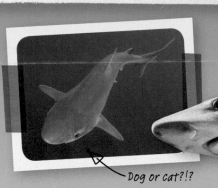

Dog or cat?!?

Topes are ovoviviparous, giving birth to litters of up to 50 pups.

FISHERMEN'S FAVORITE

Topes are very popular among fishermen, as their flesh, liver oil, fins, and skin are all valuable. Some nations, like Australia and New Zealand, have management plans to make sure the tope populations stay healthy. Sadly, most nations do not have such plans. As a result, numbers of tope sharks have been steadily decreasing in the past few decades.

ATLANTIC WEASEL SHARK

This yellow-striped beauty is also a close cousin of the catsharks (and the hammerheads, requiems, and houndsharks), and it lives in the eastern Atlantic Ocean along the west coast of Africa. The Atlantic weasel shark *(Paragaleus pectoralis)* is viviparous and grows to be about 3 feet (1 m).

The large, elongated spots that go across the spine are called saddles.

Back has striking bright yellow stripes that fade after capture.

Large, oval-shaped eyes have nictitating membranes.

Upper lobe of tail is elongated and contains a notch.

PICKY EATERS

Atlantic weasels eat squid and octopus almost exclusively.

Mouth is small.

Snout is long.

The Chondrichthyes Chronicles

"All the News That's Fit to Swim"

VOLUME I: EARLY EDITION

DATE: LONG, LONG AGO

PRICE: 50 CLAMS

IT'S A SHARK-EATS-AMPHIBIAN-EATS-FISH WORLD (OR WAS)

Spectacular fossil shows 290-million-year-old food chain

By Cosmo M. Digg

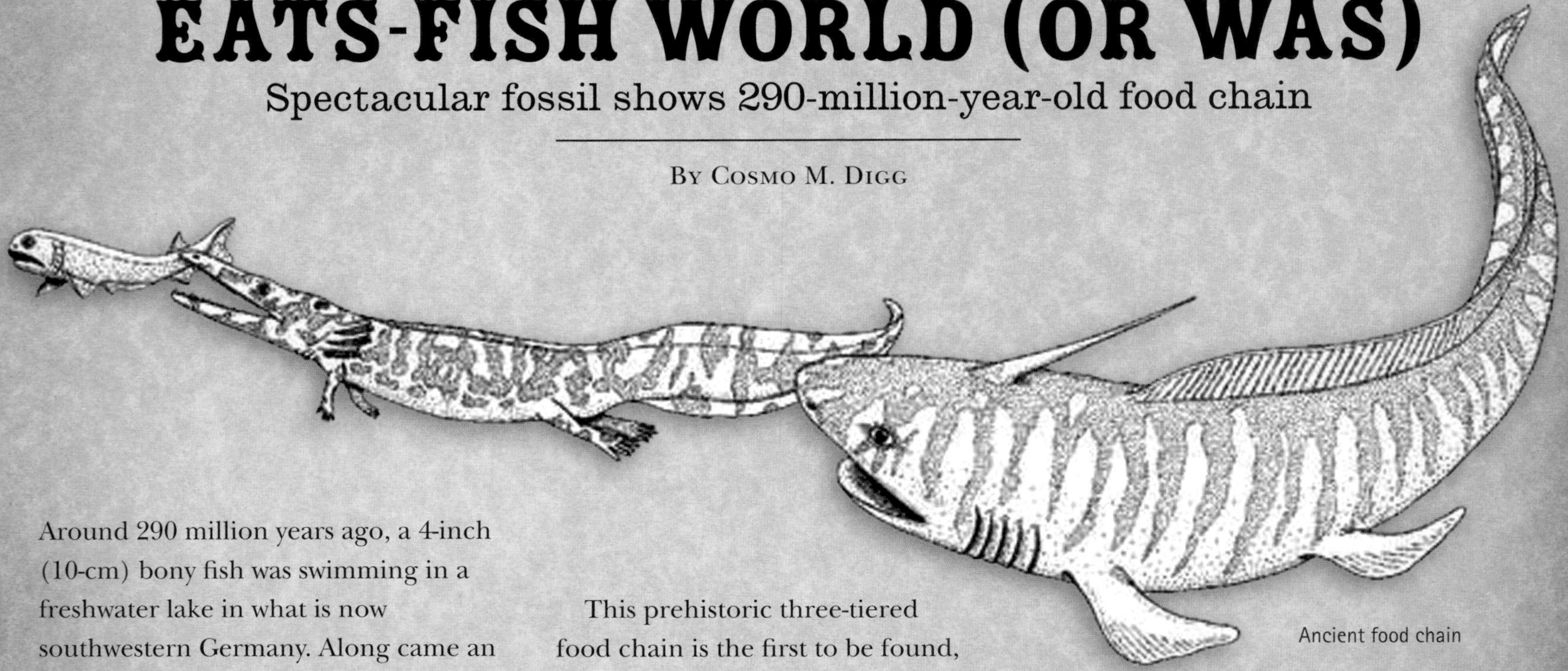

Around 290 million years ago, a 4-inch (10-cm) bony fish was swimming in a freshwater lake in what is now southwestern Germany. Along came an 8-inch (20-cm) crocodile-like amphibian called a temnospondyl, which snapped up the fish. Its belly full, the temnospondyl continued on its way, only to be swallowed by a 20-inch (50-cm) shark! Soon thereafter the shark was encased in sand or silt.

This prehistoric three-tiered food chain is the first to be found, giving scientists a never-before-seen look at prehistoric aquatic life. Dating to the late Permian period, the temnospondyl may have been a precursor to the crocodile, which did not yet exist. This is the only example ever of a shark eating an amphibian.

No other ancient or modern sharks are known to do so. Scientists hope to glean even more about sharks' early ancestors through fossil finds like this one.

Ancient food chain

BEWARE

MERCURY IN SEAFOOD!

EAT SMALL BONY FISH!

The Joint Association of Worldwide Sharks wants you to be healthy, SO DON'T EAT US!

J.A.W.S. WANTS YOU TO KNOW:

- Mercury is a naturally occurring element that is released into the air through industrial pollution.

- Mercury then falls into rivers and oceans and becomes methylmercury, which humans aren't meant to consume.

- Methylmercury accumulates over time in the bodies of fish that eat it. The older the fish or the higher you go on the marine food chain, the more mercury you'll find.

- Sharks are at the top of the marine food chain.

- Don't eat sharks.

- Fish and seafood are still great ways to get heart-healthy Omega-3 fatty acids (just don't eat SHARKS).

- Don't eat sharks. We're really not that tasty.

Get your seafood health benefits from other sea creatures, like tilapia, salmon, and farm-raised shrimp.

Eat salmon.

DON'T EAT SHARKS.

Thank you,

J.A.W.S.

With extra support from Swordfish Worldwide and SNoTT (Say No To Tuna)

SHARK-AND-CHIPS A PROBLEM IN S.A. AND AUSTRALIA

Five shark species suffering from South African export

By Amy E. Watson

Capetown, South Africa, 2007—Five shark species native to the waters around South Africa are threatened due to the large amounts of shark meat exported to Australia for fish-and-chips. Conservation groups are calling for the closer monitoring and regulation of demersal (bottom) fishing around South Africa to protect smoothhound, tope, copper, dusky, and white-spotted smoothhound sharks.

It seems that these five species are mostly caught by bottom trawlers as bycatch. And because bycatch isn't regulated or monitored very closely, nobody is quite sure how many sharks are taken each year. Conservation groups hope that close monitoring and management will help protect these sharks whose populations are declining worldwide.

WEIRD OR WHAT?

The ocean is a weird and wonderful place, filled with weird and wonderful creatures. And while you may think "gray, sleek, and toothy" when you think "shark," after reading these next pages you'll realize that sharks come in lots of varieties.

ANGEL SHARK

This "heavenly" creature looks like a normal-shaped shark that's had a nasty encounter with a steamroller. It's also called a monkfish or sanddevil.

BOTTOM DWELLER

These docile animals live in coastal waters down to depths of 3,300 feet (1,006 m). They spend their days hanging out on the seabed waiting for dinner to come their way. They do perk up at night, however, and may travel over 5 miles (8 km) when on the hunt.

HOOD ORNAMENT

In the 16th century angel sharks were given the name "monkfish" because the shape of their heads look like the hood on a monk's cloak.

The eyes and spiracles (for breathing) are on the top of the head and the mouth is at the front.

Teeth are sharp and jagged.

There are fleshy barbels on the snout.

Body is flat, and pectoral fins are broad and winglike.

The lower lobe of the tail is longer than the upper lobe—a look unique to angel sharks.

WALK THIS WAY

Besides swimming, angel sharks can "crawl" on the seafloor by undulating their pectoral fins.

A shark doing the crawl

VITAL STATS

Angel Shark (*Squatina dumeril* and its Pacific cousin, *Squatina californica*)

Length: *up to 6 ft (1.8 m)*

Weight: *90 lbs (40 kg)*

Reproduction: *ovoviviparous*

Diet: *small bony fish, crustaceans, rays, squid, mollusks*

Conservation status: *from not at risk to critically endangered*

VITAL STATS
Frilled Shark (Chlamydoselachus anguineus)

Length: _6 ft (1.8 m)_

Reproduction: _ovoviviparous_

Diet: _small bony fish, smaller sharks, cephalopods_

Conservation status: _near threatened_

FRILLED SHARK

The frilled shark is truly a living fossil. With six gill slits instead of the usual five, an eel-like body shape, a primitive lateral line, and one dorsal fin, the frilled shark has features no longer found in modern sharks. Not much else is known about this rare deepwater dweller, which makes its home from 175 to almost 5,000 feet (50 to 1,500 m) deep.

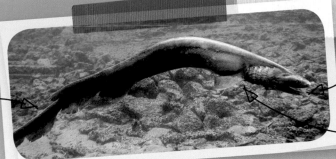

This long, slender shark could pass for an eel.

The three-cusped (or frilled) teeth resemble those of sharks that lived 400 million years ago.

Pectoral fins are short and round; skin is brown.

BRAMBLE SHARK

Look at—but don't touch—the bramble shark, or you'll be in for a sharp reminder that "brambles" are prickly spines. You'll find them in abundance on this shark.

UNCOMMON CREATURE

Bramble sharks are a type of dogfish shark. They live in the deep sea—down to 3,000 feet (900 m)—and rarely come into contact with humans. Because bramble sharks are so uncommon, little is known about them.

SECOND DEFENSE

Not only will the brambles keep predators at bay, so will the foul-smelling mucus that covers this shark's body.

VITAL STATS
Bramble Shark (Echinorhinus brucus)

Length: _7 ft (2 m); females are notably bigger than males_

Reproduction: _ovoviviparous_

Diet: _small bony fish, smaller sharks, cephalopods_

Conservation status: _data deficient_

The skin is thin and delicate and covered in sharp spines, except along the back.

The dark brownish-purple skin is lighter on the belly.

Gives birth to litters of 15 to 25 pups.

GREENLAND SHARK

A member of the dogfish shark family, the Greenland shark is a large, sluggish shark that lives in the cold waters near Canada, Greenland, and Scandinavia.

Snout is short and rounded.

Body is stout.

A SHARK WITH SORE EYES

Long, thin crustaceans called copepods dangle from the corneas of the Greenland shark. Several copepods can be attached to each cornea, which damages the shark's eyes, eventually leading to blindness. However, the sharks don't seem to mind. They hunt mostly by smell.

Eyes are, well, occupied.

Nostrils are very sensitive.

VITAL STATS
Goblin Shark (Mitsukurina owstoni)

Length:	6 to 15 ft (1.8 to 4.5 m)
Weight:	over 400 lbs (180 kg)
Reproduction:	thought to be ovoviviparous
Diet:	small bony fish, squid, crustaceans
Conservation status:	data deficient

GOBLIN SHARK

These creatures have an odd-shaped head and an unusually long, beak-like snout. To top it off, the teeth at the front of their mouths look like fangs, and their bodies are soft and flabby.

ELUSIVE GHOST

This looker has never been observed in its natural habitat. Everything we know about it has been deduced from about 50 accidental catches. It is known that goblins live at depths of 900 to 4,000 feet (275 to 1,200 m).

The lower lobe of the tail is underdeveloped.

The pointy snout looks like a horn, but is actually soft.

PORT JACKSON SHARK

Named for an inlet in Australia, Port Jackson sharks are one of just eight species that make up the bullhead sharks (named for their broad heads and ridges above their eyes).

VITAL STATS
Port Jackson Shark
(Heterodontus portusjacksoni)

Length: *up to 5 ft (1.5 m), although usually much smaller; females are larger than males*

Weight: *over 400 lbs (180 kg)*

Reproduction: *ovoviviparous*

Diet: *fish, mollusks, crustaceans, sea urchins*

Conservation status: *vulnerable*

NAME GAME

These sharks are also known as horn sharks, pigfish, and bulldog sharks.

Sharp front teeth are good for spearing prey; back teeth are blunt for crushing shells.

The first and second dorsal fins have spines.

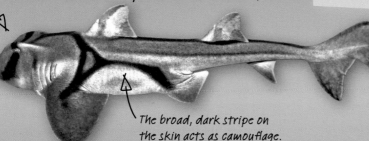

The broad, dark stripe on the skin acts as camouflage.

SLUMBER PARTY

It's not uncommon to find large groups of Port Jacksons tucked into their "seabed," taking an afternoon nap.

TERRIBLE TRINKETS

Port Jackson sharks are sometimes killed for their spines, which are used to make jewelry.

SAWSHARK

There's no missing the big, saw-toothed snout of the sawshark.

The saw can grow to be 3 ft (1 m) long.

Extremely sensitive barbels poke around for prey hiding in the seafloor.

VITAL STATS
Sawshark (Pristiophorus cirratus)

Length: *up to 4 ft (1.2 m)*

Weight: *less than 20 lbs (9 kg)*

Reproduction: *ovoviviparous*

Diet: *small bony fish, crustaceans, squid, octopus*

Conservation status: *vulnerable*

DEEP DIGGERS

Sawsharks are found in warm waters at depths of 125 feet (40 m) or below. Despite their scary-looking saws, these sharks aren't aggressive. They like to stir up the seabed in search of small fish and crabs.

The Chondrichthyes Chronicles

"All the News That's Fit to Swim"

VOLUME 1: EARLY EDITION

DATE: MONDAY

PRICE: 50 CLAMS

CONSERVATION COUP

First angel shark pups born in captivity

By Gabriel Seraphim

It wasn't just California dreamin', it was a real-life blessed event! In September 2007, the Aquarium of the Bay in San Francisco welcomed into the world the first-ever Pacific angel shark pup to be born in captivity. At birth, the tot measured 9.2 inches (23.4 cm) and weighed 4.5 ounces (127.6 g).

The Aquarium of the Bay is the only aquarium in the United States to exhibit angel sharks regularly, and has two adult angel sharks in its collection, along with its new bundle of joy. The aquarium does field research to find out how and where angel sharks live. A shark-tagging program has also been implemented to show how these sharks fit in to the local ecosystem and what actions need to be taken to ensure that they thrive.

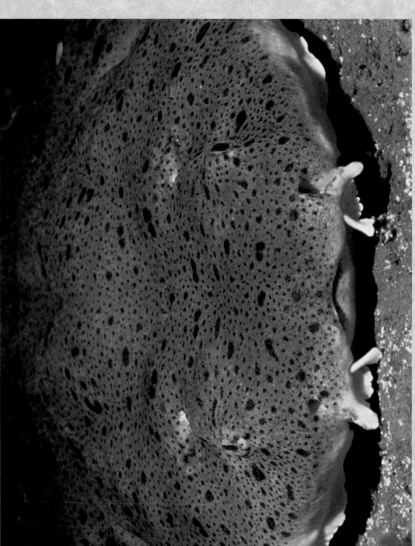

The bottom-dwelling angel shark is ovoviviparous.

15 MINUTES OF FAME

In January 2007 the usually elusive frilled shark made it into the headlines and even got its own video on YouTube.

By Slim Sharkakowa

Officials at the Awashima Marine Park outside Tokyo, Japan, came running when they got a call from local fishermen who had found a "strange eel-like fish with razor-sharp teeth." The 5-foot (1.5-m) female frilled shark was then captured by park staff, who

feared for its health. The shark was placed in a saltwater tank and filmed and photographed. So rare was the catch that it even made the news. Unfortunately, the "frill" was short-lived, as the shark died within a few hours, most likely because it was sick when it surfaced.

Turning Japanese

The frilled shark seems partial to Japan: The rarely seen species was discovered in Japanese waters in the 19th century.

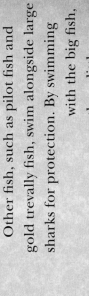

This shark was named for its frilled teeth.

HITCHHIKERS' GUIDE TO THE OCEANS

By Skipjack Kerouac

Remoras are small fish that literally hitch a ride with others. They use ridged suckers on their heads to clamp on to large sharks. It's not that they can't swim—they're just lazy. They do return the favor, however, by eating irritating skin parasites off of their hosts.

Other fish, such as pilot fish and gold trevally fish, swim alongside large sharks for protection. By swimming with the big fish, these little fellows are protected from predators. It may seem like a risky strategy, but the small guys are quick enough to stay out of the jaws of their traveling buddies.

Fish taking cover under the belly of a white shark

GENTLE GIANTS

Whale sharks, basking sharks, and megamouth sharks are the largest non-bony fish in the sea and the largest of the sharks. These lumbering lummoxes might look intimidating, but they are actually serene, plankton-eating fish. They quietly go about their business, sucking in massive amounts of water, filling up on tiny plankton, krill, and small fish that float near the surface.

The head is kind of flat, and the eyes are small.

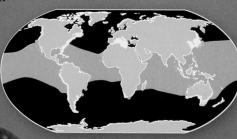

This is a person, not a shark.

The pattern of yellowish stripes and dots is unique for each shark. It's like their fingerprint.

VITAL STATS
Whale Shark (Rhincodon typus)

Length: about 45 ft (13.7 m)

Weight: up to 36 tons (33 metric tons)

Reproduction: ovoviviparous

Diet: zooplankton, krill, squid

Back is dark bluish-gray, and belly is white.

Large mouth is terminal, meaning it's in front of the snout, not underneath it.

Both males and females have a white band where an upper lip would be (if sharks had lips).

FILTER FEEDERS

All three of these sharks are filter feeders. They swim with their mouths open and take in vast quantities of water—and the tiny life-forms that live there. Then they move the water through their gills—either by letting it flow past or by pumping it out. Here's where it gets interesting: Inside their gills are special structures called gill rakers, which act as tiny hooks that hang on to the tiny food as the water gets pushed out. When the water's gone, the shark swallows what was caught in the gill rakers. Delish!

VITAL STATS
Megamouth Shark (Megachasma pelagios)

Length: up to 18 ft (5.5 m) (females are larger)

Weight: up to 2,000 lbs (907 kg)

Reproduction: ovoviviparous

Diet: zooplankton, krill, small fish

The basking shark has a large head and skinny snout.

Eyes are small.

The structure of the mouth can be seen when it opens its yap.

VITAL STATS
Basking Shark (Cetorhinus maximus)

Length: up to 33 ft (10 m)

Weight: 4.5 tons (4 metric tons)

Reproduction: ovoviviparous

Diet: zooplankton, krill, small fish

The whale shark's gaping maw can be 4 ft (1 m) across!

This guy has more than 3,000 ti... in that enormous mouth, altho... shark doesn't chew its food.

WHALE SHARK

The whale shark is the largest non-bony fish in the sea, and the largest shark. It does not take top honors in the whole marine kingdom, however. The blue whale is the largest marine animal alive today at 110 feet (33 m) long.

DEEP DIVERS

The Shark Research Institute (SRI) runs the oldest, largest study of whale sharks in the world, and has discovered many things about the lives of these giant fish. Although their coloration suggests that whale sharks spend their lives near the surface, SRI's satellite tags revealed that the sharks dive to depths of 2,500 feet (762 m), sometimes several times a day. Two whale sharks tagged by SRI off East Africa dived to 3,937 feet (1,200 m)!

STANDING TALL

Whale sharks will swim with their mouths open to get their fill of plankton, but they'll also suck in water like a giant undersea vacuum (sometimes while hanging vertically in the water).

FRIENDLY FISH

Whale sharks don't mind boats or divers. Coupled with the fact that they often linger near the surface, these giant fish are a favorite among scuba divers and underwater photographers.

BASKING SHARK

The basking shark is perhaps best adapted for filter feeding, since its gill slits encircle its enormous noggin almost entirely. Huge gill slits mean more gill rakers—and more trapped lunch.

The liver runs the entire length of the abdominal cavity and contains a LOT of squalene (necessary for buoyancy).

There are hundreds of tiny teeth in the mouth, but they're somewhat useless (plankton doesn't need to be chewed).

Basking sharks are trusting slowpokes—which means they're very easy to catch. They're a favorite among fishermen for their meat, skin, liver, cartilage, and fins. As a result, basking shark populations are falling, and many countries (including the U.S., Great Britain, and Malta) now protect these docile creatures.

SHARK MYTH
Some people believe that basking sharks hibernate in the winter. This isn't true. Scientists believe that in winter they simply swim and eat at lower depths.

BASKING BUNCH
These sharks are one of the few social shark species (say *that* ten times fast), and can be found in groups of up to one hundred.

THIRSTY?
This giant can filter 2,500 tons (2,268 metric tons) of water every hour.

BIG BABY
Basking pups hatch inside the mother's body and grow until they're about 6 feet (2 m) long! Like all shark pups, once they're born, they're on their own.

MEGAMOUTH SHARK

This shark is a mega mystery. The first megamouth was caught accidentally by the U.S. Navy in 1976, off the coast of Hawaii. It had never been seen before that. And since then, these shy behemoths have remained elusive. Fewer than 40 have been spotted or caught in oceans around the world.

It has a large head and blunt snout.

Dark gray back fades to a light gray or white belly.

There are fifty rows of small, hooklike teeth in the mouth.

VERY SPECIAL SHARK
A whole new family, genus, and species had to be created for the megamouth because it is so unique.

A WHALE OF A PREDATOR
It seems the megamouth's only predator (besides man) is the sperm whale.

UP AND DOWN
Only one megamouth shark has ever been successfully tagged. Researchers tracked it for two days, and found that it spent much of the night about 50 feet (15 m) below the surface of the water, but sank deeper than 500 feet (152 m) during the day. It was probably following prey.

The Chondrichthyes Chronicles

"All the News That's Fit to Swim"

VOLUME I: EARLY EDITION

DATE: YOUR BIRTHDAY

PRICE: 50 CLAMS

A WHALE SHARK FOR A GOLDFISH

Whale sharks in captivity taking U.S. aquarium by storm

BY MUDDY DORSAL

Atlanta, Georgia, 2007—Four whale sharks are the star attraction at the largest indoor aquarium in the United States: The Georgia Aquarium in Atlanta, Georgia. Trixie, Alice, Yushan, and Taroko, draw people of all ages and scientists from around the world to their giant home.

But keeping such incredibly large fish in captivity is proving to be extremely difficult for the Aquarium. Trixie and Alice's original tank mates—Ralph and Norton—died in 2007.

million gallons (23.8 million liters)—can accommodate this behavior. Some conservationists are questioning the benefit of keeping whale sharks in captivity at all.

That said, there is a terrific benefit to Georgia's program: Their whale sharks were all rescued from a thriving whaling industry in Asia. If the foursome had been left in Asian waters, they might have fallen victim to a hunting expedition.

Visitors marvel at the whale sharks. Scientists have discovered that whale sharks dive thousands of feet each day in the open ocean. No manmade enclosure—even one that holds 6.3

TOURISM—A GOOD THING FOR WHALE SHARKS?

By Watson R. Beach

Ningaloo, Western Australia—Ecotourism has helped Australian researchers compile more data on whale sharks than ever before. Biologists at the Ningaloo Marine Park in Western Australia began a study of the local whale shark populations in 1995. Over the course of a decade, they photographed the sharks that came to the park every year. They also collected photos from the thousands of ecotourists that visit Ningaloo.

By analyzing more than five thousand images, the scientists learned that the local whale shark population seems to be increasing. It also seems that many of the sharks were return visitors. By including images collected by tourists, the Ningaloo researchers widened their data pool, allowing them a more complete look at the whale sharks' behavior and health. This is a novel approach to research, one which may help shark populations around the globe.

NO SOUP FOR YOU!
"Finning" on the rise, and threatening sharks worldwide

By Julia A.J. Williams

Imagine walking down the street and having someone scoop you up, cut off your legs, and throw you back onto the sidewalk. Cruel and unusual, right? Well, sadly, it's not so unusual for many sharks.

"Finning" is the practice of cutting the fins off of a shark and throwing its body back into the ocean—sometimes while the shark is still alive. Without its fins a shark can't swim, and so will either drown or become lunch for other sea creatures. The fins are then frozen or dried, and quickly sent to China for their use in a prized delicacy: shark-fin soup.

The soup is very expensive—usually more than $100 per bowl—and is a sign of wealth and success in China. It's often served at important banquets. And with a rapidly growing Chinese middle class, more and more people can afford the soup, which means more and more sharks are being hunted. Scientists estimate that 38 to 100 million sharks are killed each year for their fins. And no shark is safe: All species are targeted, with basking sharks, white sharks, and tiger sharks bearing the brunt.

Not only is the practice barbaric and wasteful, many scientists believe it is contributing to the frightening decline in shark populations

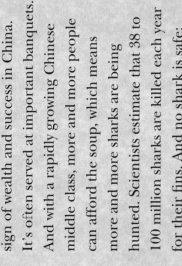

Shark fins laying out to dry

around the world. Many governments have banned finning, but fishermen are simply going farther out to sea, where the regulations are harder to enforce. If we continue at this rate, we risk throwing the marine ecosystem into a tailspin from which it may never recover.

CARPETSHARKS

The carpetsharks (or Orectolobiformes if you want to be fancy) are an extremely diverse group of sharks, ranging from the one-foot (30-cm) barbelthroat to the world's largest fish: the 60-foot (18-m) whale shark.

AREA RUG

The carpetsharks are so named because almost all members of this group live on the seafloor, like a denticled rug. They tend to be sluggish and prefer to wait for prey to come to them.

EPAULETTE SHARK

This small, smooth operator (*Hemiscyllium ocellatum*) is named for the large distinctive spots where its shoulders would be . . . if it had shoulders.

Dark identifying spots are found above the pectoral fins.

Snout has short barbels.

Tail is long and thick.

Teeth are pointy, but can flatten when feeding on hard shells.

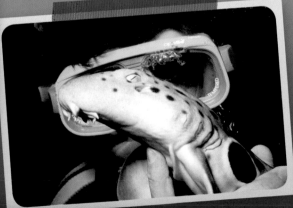

HUMAN-FRIENDLY

Epaulettes often swim in very shallow water, making them extremely easy to catch. In fact, a person can simply reach down and pick the fish out of the water. That would, of course, be traumatizing to the animal—not to mention rude—so I don't recommend it.

BROWNBANDED BAMBOOSHARK

Chiloscyllium punctatum—aka the brownbanded bambooshark or brown-spotted catshark—is banded only as a juvenile. Once the shark reaches maturity, the bands fade to a solid brown color.

This shark is oviparous.

This shark grows to be about 3 ft (1m) long.

Pectoral fins are broad.

Rounded snout has short barbels.

OXYGEN? WHO NEEDS IT?

The brownbanded bambooshark is unique in that it can spend extended periods of time in shallow tidal pools, where there's little oxygen to be had. This bambooshark simply shuts down nonessential processes to conserve the oxygen already in its bloodstream.

Carpetshark cousins: an epaulette shark and a whitespotted bambooshark.

VITAL STATS
Carpetsharks (Order Orectolobiformes)

Length: most average 2 to 3 ft (0.5 to 1 m)

Weight: average up to 500 lbs (227 kg) (not counting the mammoth whale shark)

Reproduction: oviparous or ovoviviparous

Diet: most eat small fish, squid, and crustaceans, with larger sharks also taking larger fish and small marine mammals

Conservation status: many species are threatened, vulnerable, or endangered

MYTHBUSTING

You've heard the myth that if a shark stops swimming it dies, right? While that's true for some sharks, it's not true for all: Carpetsharks can pump water over their gills while they sit still at the bottom of the sea.

CARPETSHARKS

Carpetsharks are found around the world. Some live in inches of water; others at a few thousand feet. Most of these sharks like to lay low on the ocean floor and wait for prey to come to them.

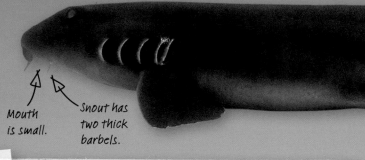

Head is broad.

Mouth is small.

Snout has two thick barbels.

TASSELLED WOBBEGONG

Yes, this is really the name of a shark. In fact, the wobbegongs are a whole family of sharks: the Orectolobidae family, which has seven species.

WOE IS ME!

Also known as the bearded wobbegong, this tasseled shark (*Eucrossorhinus dasypogon*) spends its days resting in and around coral reefs, and hunts at night. It can grow to be 9 feet (3 m) long!

Two nasal barbels are also fringed.

SECRET SUCKER

While this shark waits for prey to swim by, the color pattern on its body—and those fabulous tassels—make it almost impossible to spot. When a fish, crustacean, or worm gets close enough, the wobbegong sucks the victim in.

Chin is covered in dermal lobes—the "tassels"—that act as camouflage.

Teeth are fanglike and extremely sharp.

NURSE SHARK

Nurse sharks *(Ginglymostoma cirratum)* are large carpetsharks that reach lengths of 9 feet (3 m). These sluggish fish lurk around coral reefs to depths of 250 feet (76 m) during the day, coming shallower at night to hunt lobsters, crab, squid, and small fish.

Body is long and stout.

The skin is grayish brown. Juveniles often have black spots.

CREATURE OF HABIT

After a night of serious hunting, a nurse shark will often return to the same cave or resting spot day after day. It will lie still for most of the day, conserving energy for its evening hunt.

LAZY SUSANS

The nurse shark is a sluggish swimmer, even when it's on the hunt. In fact, sometimes the shark doesn't even swim, but instead crawls around on its pectoral fins. To catch fish that are moving too quickly, the shark can suck in water—and anything delicious that may come with it.

Tail is long, often a full half of the shark's length.

Spots are dark brown on yellowish-brown skin.

ZEBRA SHARK

You would think that zebra sharks *(Stegostoma fasciatum)* would be striped, wouldn't you? Well, they are—but only when they're young. As zebra sharks grow, their stripes break up into a pattern of dark brown spots. They're sometimes (confusingly) called leopard sharks.

The Chondrichthyes Chronicles

"All the News That's Fit to Swim"

VOLUME I: EARLY EDITION

DATE: MONDAY

PRICE: 50 CLAMS

SHARK HANGS ON FOR DEAR LIFE

Small shark bites man's leg and won't let go

By NIBBLES CUSPLET

Sydney, Australia, 2004—Twenty-two-year-old Luke Tresoglavic was enjoying a day of snorkeling at a reef off Caves Beach, near Newcastle, when a carpetshark latched onto him. The small shark bit his shin and refused to let go. After trying to shake it loose (to no avail), Tresoglavic swam 1,000 feet (304 m) to shore to get help.

After fellow beachgoers tried and failed to break him free, Tresoglavic got in his car—shark and all—and drove to the surf clubhouse where lifeguards took over. They flushed the shark's gills with freshwater (something saltwater fish do NOT like), and the shark eventually loosened its grip. Tresoglavic suffered a few puncture wounds to his shin, but was not seriously injured. The shark (later identified as *Brachaelurus waddi*, or blind shark) died later that afternoon.

Tresoglavic and his "friend"

MARATHON LABOR FOR SHARK

Female shark becomes first wobbegong to give birth in captivity

By VENUS SALTWATER

England, October 1999—Eleven days of labor would have most moms calling for relief, but not Gaynor, a wobbegong at the Blackpool Sea Life Centre in Blackpool, England. Researchers noticed the shark was pregnant about four weeks before the blessed event, and moved her to a quarantined tank (lest her newborns become lunch for some of her usual tank mates).

Gaynor's pups hatched from their eggs inside her body before she gave birth. Staff members had carried out an ultrasound and suspected that approximately 20 pups would be born. On October 7, the first two arrived, looking like mini replicas of their mother. Twenty-four hours passed before another two pups were born. The delay took researchers by surprise.

Approximately two pups were born each day for eleven days, for a grand total of twenty-three young wobbegongs.

Researchers believe that such a staggered birth would probably help survival rates in the wild, where a large group of newborns would attract unwanted attention.

Already equipped with sharp teeth, the mini wobbegongs hungrily gobbled their first meal of crustaceans, squid, and eel. Babies and mother are doing well.

WANTED: NURSE SHARKS FOR ANTHRAX RESEARCH

2003—Due to the sturdiness of shark antibodies, researchers are using nurse sharks to develop ways to detect and treat anthrax and other infectious diseases. Nurse-shark antibodies are extremely sensitive but very hardy, which makes them ideal for use in battlefield situations.

Studies have already proven that shark antibodies can be used to detect the presence of anthrax. Now researchers are hoping to develop treatments and vaccines for this highly contagious and dangerous disease. So if you're a nurse shark and want to help with this research, please contact us immediately. Details are below.

WHERE: National Aquarium, Baltimore, Maryland

WHEN: Ongoing

WHAT: Here's what will happen:

- Scientists will gently take you out of your tank and place you in a smaller tank that has some anesthetic in it. You won't be put under; you'll just feel *really* relaxed.

- Anthrax proteins will be injected into your bloodstream. These proteins will **not** cause disease. They will simply trigger your immune system to create antibodies (cells that attack germs).

- Once a month for three months, you'll be given a booster shot to keep your immune system pumping out the antibodies. Some blood will be collected for study.

- You'll save the world.

COMPENSATION: We will provide meals of lobster and shrimp, and will do free parasite removal while you're in our facility.

Nurse sharks of all ages are invited.

BLACK AND WHITE

Now we're getting into bigger, mightier sharks, so stay with me. While none of these magnificent sharks—from the requiem family—hunt humans, they are still large, powerful animals.

BLACKTIP REEF SHARK

Not to be confused with the blacktip shark, the blacktip reef shark (*Carcharhinus melanopterus*) stays close to reefs and shorelines.

SHALLOW NURSERIES

Blacktip reef sharks are viviparous and give birth in shallow waters. Their litters (of up to 10 live pups) tend to stay in shallow water for a few years before venturing into the depths.

CALMER COUSIN

The blacktip reef shark is not quite as aggressive as its blacktip and oceanic whitetip cousins, although it may nip at the feet of swimmers wading near coral reefs or mangrove swamps.

Like its cousin the blacktip shark, the blacktip reef shark has dorsal and tail fins tipped with black markings.

The rounded dorsal fin has a white tip.

They grow to be about 6 ft (1.8 m) long.

Eyes are oval in shape.

Eyes are small.

OCEANIC WHITETIP SHARK

Carcharhinus longimanus cruises the open ocean. It can grow to be 7.5 feet (2.3 m) long, and has a bad rep for attacking survivors of shipwrecks and plane crashes.

CHOW DOWN

Food is scarce in the open ocean, so oceanic whitetips eat almost anything: marine mammals, seabirds, fish, crustaceans, turtles, and squid. They particularly like tuna, and will swim through tuna schools with their mouths open.

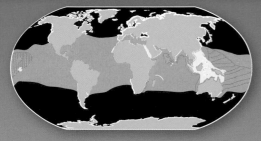

Requiems can be found around the world. Most prefer shallow waters near shore, but a few species thrive in the open ocean.

↗ The eyes are small.

↖ The stout body ends in a pointy snout.

BLACKTIP SHARK

Blacktip sharks *(Carcharhinus limbatus)* are found in shallow waters around the world. They tend to hang out near river estuaries (although they don't swim upriver like their cousin the bull shark).

↘ Blacktips grow to be about 5 ft (1.5 m) long, and weigh around 50 lbs (23 kg).

WHITETIP REEF SHARK

Smaller and more docile than its oceanic cousin, the whitetip reef shark *(Triaenodon obesus)* can be found in coastal reefs. These curious sharks are tenacious hunters, known to chase prey relentlessly, sometimes in packs.

THICK-SKINNED

Whitetip reef sharks have very thick skin, which helps them barrel through sharp reefs while on the chase. These sharks are known to seriously damage reefs with their rambunctious behavior.

Whitetip reefs are viviparous, and give birth to litters of up to four pups.

NIGHT LIFE

The whitetip reef shark is a nocturnal hunter. During the day groups of sharks find a favorite cave and rest. Some groups are so large that they pile up on each other while resting.

Dorsal fin and tail have bright white spots.

Adults can be about 5 ft (1.5 m) long.

Oval eyes are protected by ridges.

Blunt snout has two barbels.

YELLOW AND BLUE

Here are some more requiem cousins from around the world. These sharks like warm waters, with many favoring the seas around coral reefs.

SPINNER SHARK

This shark comes by its name honestly. *Carcharhinus brevipinna* hunts by spinning vertically through schools of fish and grabbing everything it can. The spinner is known to spin right out of the water!

Sometimes has dark spots on its dorsal fins and tail, and can often be confused with the blacktip shark.

Body is narrow and grows up to 8 ft (2.4 m) long.

Teeth are sharp and needle-shaped.

The viviparous spinner gives birth to litters of up to 10 live pups.

BLUE SHARK

Prionace glauca is the marathoner of the sea, traveling great distances each year. The blue shark is a fierce hunter, and lives down to 1,200 feet (366 m).

Long and pointy snout

Eyes are large and round.

Pectoral fins are extremely long.

Gets its name from its rich, blue color.

BIG, BAD, BLUE

Although it is known to be a somewhat sluggish swimmer, the blue shark has a reputation for being involved in accidents with humans, especially divers.

NO ORDINARY SHARK

Although blue sharks are some of the most common in the open ocean, they are not ordinary by any means. The females are viviparous and can carry litters of more than 120 pups!

SILKY SHARK

This is an active, quick-swimming shark that prefers warm waters around the world. The silky shark (*Carcharhinus falciformis*) grows to be more than 10 feet (3 m) long.

Denticles are very small and tightly packed, creating the smoothest surface of any shark skin.

Eyes are round and large.

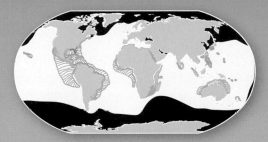

TUNA, ANYONE?

Silky sharks have got a *serious* tuna habit. In fact, they are sometimes called "net-eaters" because of their tendency to rip apart fishing nets when trying to get their tuna fix.

LEMON SHARK

Named for its yellow-tan color, the lemon shark, *Negaprion brevirostris*, grows to be more than 10 feet (3.4 m) long.

The snout is short and blunt.

The two dorsal fins are almost equal in size, and set far back on the body.

VITAL STATS
Requiem Sharks (Family Carcharhinidae)

Length: from the 2-ft (60-cm) Atlantic sharpnose to the 18-ft (5-m) tiger shark

Reproduction: most requiems are viviparous, but some are ovoviviparous

Diet: bony fish, marine mammals, crustaceans, squid, and other sharks

IN THE SHALLOWS

Adult lemon sharks rarely go into deep water, preferring mangrove swamps, coral reefs, and even river estuaries. Their favorite meals include seabirds, bony fish, crustaceans, rays, and even smaller sharks.

The Chondrichthyes Chronicles

"All the News That's Fit to Swim"

VOLUME I: EARLY EDITION   DATE: TOMORROW   PRICE: 50 CLAMS

CAN SHARKS HELP THE NAVY GO GREEN?

A new, environmentally friendly coating for ships that's modeled after sharks' skin is under development for use by the U.S. Navy

By Lt. Elasmo P. Sharke

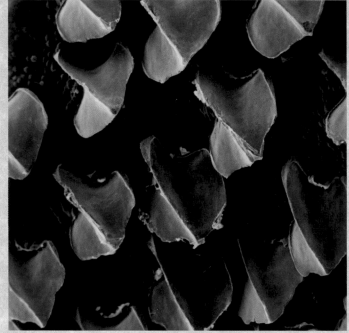

Shark denticles, shown here, are highly specialized.

Big ships get slowed down by algae, barnacles, and all manner of hangers-on. These unwanted passengers create drag, which then jacks up fuel costs (at an estimated price tag of $50 million per year). Cleaning off the stowaways is also a costly and time-consuming business. At present, special paints are applied to the hulls of ships to kill organisms that latch on, but the paints are harmful to other sea creatures and ocean wildlife. So researchers have turned to nature for a better solution.

Despite spending their entire lives underwater, sharks aren't burdened with barnacles, even though many other sea dwellers are. This lack of cling-ons comes down to the design of the sharks' skin. The skin's dermal denticles move and flex as the animals swim, making it hard for uninvited guests to latch on.

Using a combination of rubber and plastic, researchers at the University of Florida have created a coating for ships that comes close to replicating sharkskin. The final product is a few years away, but if all goes according to plan, an eco-friendly coating could soon replace toxic paints.

THE NAME'S BOND, SHARK BOND

They may not drink martinis, but blue sharks could soon be part of the real-life spy game

By Ian Flounder

In a project funded by the Pentagon, researchers are studying ways to use brain implants to turn sharks into "stealth spies." The idea is that a remote-controlled shark swimming on its own would be able to track enemy ships without drawing attention.

While brain implant technology may seem like the stuff of sci-fi movies, it's not as far-fetched as it sounds. A team at Boston University has already used implants in the olfactory center of a spiny dogfish's brain to "steer" it in a tank. This was done using radio commands sent to an antenna on the shark (the antenna stood out of the water).

Radio signals, however, don't penetrate water, so the plan for the shark spies is to use sonar. Again taking a cue from nature, researchers have shaped the receiver like a remora fish. The implants and the communication devices are to be used with blue sharks, which will be released into the ocean for study. The most important part of the study will be to determine how this will affect the sharks, and if it will harm them in any way. Stay tuned.

SINKING OF USS *INDIANAPOLIS* REMEMBERED

By Edgar Waterson

The worst shark attack in history was experienced by the survivors of the USS *Indianapolis*, in 1945. Just after midnight on July 30, the *Indianapolis* was torpedoed by a Japanese submarine in the Philippine Sea. Two explosions killed about 300 men and sunk the ship in 12 minutes. The remaining 880 men were left in the open water with nothing but life vests. The first sharks arrived at dawn.

Most likely tiger sharks and oceanic whitetips, the sharks circled the men and attacked anyone who strayed from the group. They also took sailors who died from exposure and dehydration. The *Indianapolis*'s mission had been top secret, so nobody reported the ship missing, which meant that no rescue team was on its way. For four days the men struggled to survive with no food or freshwater, no protection from the sun or cold water, and no way to escape the ever-present sharks.

While popular history will have you believe that the sharks killed hundreds of men, that's not true. The vast majority of deaths were caused by exposure, desquamation (when the skin peels off in layers), and dehydration (which was made much worse by the men drinking saltwater). Still, the constant presence of the sharks haunted the men, and continues to haunt seafaring stories today.

On the fourth day, a pilot accidentally spotted the men and called for a rescue. Of the almost 900 men who fell into the sea, only 317 survived the ordeal.

The USS *Indianapolis*

HEADS, HE WINS

Hammerheads are some of the most striking fish in the sea. Their wide, flat heads set them apart from the rest of their chondrichthyes cousins. Nine known species of hammerhead exist, and while they're solitary nighttime hunters, these large fish are known to form schools of up to one hundred animals during the day.

VITAL STATS
Scalloped Hammerhead (*Sphyrna lewini*)

Length: *males up to 6 ft (1.8 m); females up to about 9 ft (3 m)*

Weight: *64 to 177 lbs (29 to 80 kg)*

Reproduction: *viviparous*

Diet: *small fish and sharks, rays, squid, and octopus*

Conservation status: *Near threatened*

Skin is gray on top, fading to white on the belly.

HAMMERHEAD SHARKS

Scalloped hammerheads swim in large groups during the day, and hunt at night. Swinging their heads from side to side as they swim, they check the waters for prey. The wide positioning of the eyes gives the shark a unique vantage point. But stick something right between their eyes and they can't see it!

Head is curved in young sharks and straight in adults, with scallops along the edge.

Teeth are curved and slim. Great hammerheads have similar teeth, except they're serrated.

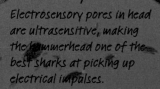

Electrosensory pores in head are ultrasensitive, making the hammerhead one of the best sharks at picking up electrical impulses.

CLOSE RELATION

The great hammerhead shark is a large, smooth-headed cousin to the scalloped hammerhead. The great hammerhead can grow to 18 feet (5.5 m) and weigh up to 1,000 lbs (454 kg).

GIRLS' NIGHT OUT?

Large schools of scalloped hammerhead females have been spotted doing a strange "dance": They nudge each other, shake their heads, and swim around in spirals. No one knows why.

LITTLE DARLINGS

Newborn hammerheads look like little replicas of their parents. They're born with their head projections bent back.

TOOL TIME

Hammerheads are partial to stingrays, which spend most of their time buried in the sand. The hammerhead swings its head around like a metal detector, and in this way, the ampullae of Lorenzini (aka electrosensory pores) can detect the ray's electrical field. Then the hammerhead uses its head like a shovel, digging up the ray. Sometimes the head is used to pin down prey while the shark takes a bite. Hammerheads are immune to the venom of the rays' tail barb.

Stingray

CHOW DOWN

TAILS, HE WINS, TOO

While the hammerhead is well known for its head, the thresher is most famous for its tail. There are three species of thresher, all of which are warm-bodied: the pelagic thresher (the smallest), the bigeye thresher (with huge eyes), and the thresher shark, which is an enormous fish reaching lengths of 23 feet (7 m) and weighing more than 1,000 lbs (454 kg).

The tail is mighty impressive, reaching lengths of up to 7 feet (2.1 m).

THRESHER SHARKS

Making up almost half of its body length, the thresher shark's single most distinguishing feature is its big, whacking tail. Found in temperate and tropical waters, threshers are pelagic sharks—meaning they like the open ocean.

Upper lobe of the caudal fin is very long, while the lower one is much shorter.

Bigeye threshers have enormous, black eyes.

MAKING A MEAL OF IT

As thresher pups develop in the uterus, they feed on bundles of unfertilized eggs. The pups can be up to 5 feet (1.5 m) long at birth.

KNOCKOUT PUNCH

Threshers hunt in groups. They use their huge tails to herd and stun prey before gobbling it up. Some claim that threshers will even flick their great tails out of the water to take down seabirds.

First dorsal fin is much bigger than the second.

Dark bluish-gray skin fades to white on the belly and under the pectoral fins.

SOUND THRASHING

A prized catch for commercial fishermen and sport anglers alike, the thresher gives as good as it gets. It will continue to thrash its deadly tail even after it's been hauled onboard a boat, so anglers beware!

DID YOU KNOW?

- Young threshers stay close to shore until they're big enough to fend for themselves in the great wide ocean.
- Threshers are one of the few sharks that can jump clear of the water like dolphins. This behavior is called breaching.
- This species is hunted by humans for its meat, liver oil, skin (which is used as leather), and fins.

The body is long and slender.

VITAL STATS
Pelagic Thresher (Alopias pelagicus)

Length: 10 ft (3 m)

Weight: 150 lbs (68 kg)

Reproduction: ovoviviparous

Diet: small bony fish, cephalopods, crustaceans, stingrays, and even the occasional seabird

Conservation status: vulnerable

Crabs are delicious.

CHOW DOWN

The Chondrichthyes Chronicles

"All the News That's Fit to Swim"

VOLUME I: EARLY EDITION

DATE: NEW YEAR'S DAY

PRICE: 50 CLAMS

CAPTIVE SHARK HAS "VIRGIN BIRTH"

When it comes to shark reproduction, DNA testing proves that the girls can go it alone

BY VIRGINIA WATERS

Omaha, Nebraska, 2007—Scientists were scratching their heads over the apparent virgin birth of a bonnethead pup at the Scott Aquarium, at the Henry Doorly Zoo in Nebraska. The mother had never had a male tank mate. So how did she find herself in the family way?

Recent developments in genetic testing have finally made it possible to answer this question. At first, scientists thought that the shark had mated with a male before her capture, then stored the sperm for three years. But tests show that the pup in question had no paternal DNA and could only have been conceived through

parthenogenesis—reproduction in which an egg cell develops into an embryo inside the mother without the egg ever being fertilized by a male.

In the wild, many species of shark are, almost literally, being fished out of the waters. Populations are declining at an alarming rate. So at first glance, parthenogenesis seems like a good thing. In reality, it's not. The reason is that offspring with less diverse DNA have a reduced ability to adapt to environmental changes or to new diseases. Over time, this could mean a slide toward extinction. Self-reproduction isn't the answer to saving sharks—conservation is.

The bundle of joy

SHARK SKIN IS WORTH ITS WEIGHT IN "GOLD"

By Epi McDermis

It's clear that sharks have that swimming thing down pat. In fact, their skin is so suited to cutting through the water quickly and effortlessly that swimwear maker Speedo developed a high-performance swimsuit made out of fabric that mimics sharkskin. Called Fastskin FSII, the suit is said to reduce drag through the water by 4 percent compared to the next-best gear.

Tiny "teeth"—called denticles—cover the surface of a shark's skin. The shape and positioning of the denticles vary across the body to manage the flow of water. With this in mind, Speedo created a full-body "skin" with different fabrics on different parts of the body.

After four years in research and development (which started at the Natural History Museum in London, England), the "sharkskin suit" was worn by athletes at the Olympic Games in Athens, Greece. For once, a "big Game" sport that does sharks proud.

NEW KIDS ON THE BLOCK . . . FOR NOW

By Priscilla C. Weed

A new species of hammerhead was discovered in 2006 off the coast of South Carolina. It's not swimmers who should be concerned, though—it's the sharks. The as-yet-unnamed species appears to be extremely rare, perhaps even at risk of extinction, and its discovery highlights the need for improved shark protection.

Nearly identical in appearance to scalloped hammerheads, this species has a genetic makeup all its own. The newcomers are thought to breed only off the shores of South Carolina, although once grown they don't seem to respect state lines, sometimes venturing into Florida and North Carolina waters.

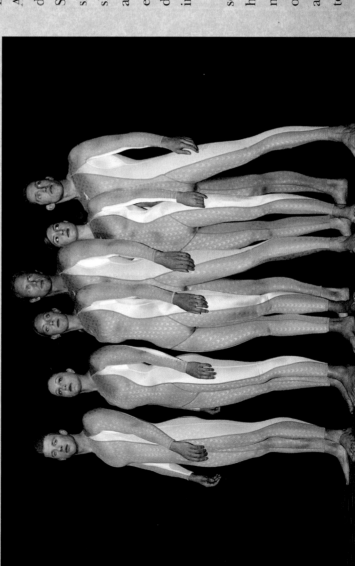

International swimmers wearing the latest sharkskin suits

MAKO OR BREAK-O

The cheetahs of the sea, makos stand out from the crowd because of their spectacular speed and agility. Along with the great white and porbeagle, the shortfin mako (and its close cousin the longfin mako) belongs to the family of mackerel sharks. (It's thought that these sharks were so named because they all share a sweet tooth for mackerel.) The mako is a sleek, spindle-shaped shark with a long, conelike snout and a crescent-shaped tail.

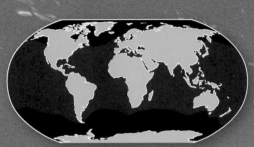

The large eyes lack a nictitating membrane.

Teeth are long, spiked, and curved, and stick out of the mouth, even when it's closed.

Because the mouth extends beyond the eyes, the mako appears to be smiling.

Fast movers like the mako breathe via ram-jet ventilation: Water is forced over the gills as the shark cuts through the water.

These are big-hearted beasts.

JUST WARMING UP

A complex network of blood vessels running through the shark's muscles passes heat to the cold blood on its way from the gills. The muscles stay warmed up like an athlete's, so this predator is primed to pounce when the time is right.

CHOW DOWN

Squid are chewy.

WRONG END OF THE FOOD CHAIN

Because it can dash, jump, and generally put up a good fight, the mako has the unfortunate distinction of being a favorite among big-game fishermen. The largest mako ever caught—in Massachusetts in 2001—weighed a whopping 1,221 lbs (554 kg).

VITAL STATS
Shortfin Mako (Isurus oxyrinchus) Longfin Mako (Isurus paucus)

Length: up to 13 ft (4 m); average is 7 to 8 ft (2 to 3 m)

Weight: can weigh over 1,000 lbs (454 kg); females are notably bigger than males, and also longer-lived

Reproduction: ovoviviparous

Diet: fish in almost all its forms, but mainly octopus, squid, mackerel, marlin, and swordfish

Conservation status: vulnerable

CONSERVATION ALERT!
Mackerel sharks were heavily fished in the North Atlantic in the 1970s, and in deep trouble by the 1980s. They have recovered to some extent, but are still classified as vulnerable.

Blue or blue-gray on its back (dorsal side) and white on its underside (ventral side)

The tail is crescent-shaped.

Like tunas, makos have single keels along the base of their tails—handy for staying the course when making sharp turns.

SPEED DEMONS
The fastest sharks in fins, these racers can clock in at speeds of up to 20 mph (32 kph) on short sprints, which makes them fearsome hunters. They're also mighty jumpers: If a mako gets caught on an angler's line, it can leap 20 feet (6 m) out of the water in an effort to break free.

IT'S A PUP-EAT-PUP WORLD
Mako pups develop inside their mothers and are nourished by the yolks of the eggs she produces. As the pups grow, they get extra nourishment by eating the other eggs—or even the developed pups—that are their womb-mates. The term for this behavior is oophagy. Mako moms then give birth to two live pups, each around 28 inches (71 cm) long.

>>HOT-BODIED
Contrary to popular belief, not all sharks are cold-bodied. Makos, like their close kin the white, thresher, and porbeagle sharks, are warm-bodied, which means they can keep their temps up even when swimming in cool water. This trait is shared with mammals, birds, and a few fast fish, such as the tuna.

MORE MACKERELS

Here are two more cousins from the mackerel family. These guys are also spindle-shaped, and they're very successful predators.

PORBEAGLE SHARK

The porbeagle's name is a combo of "porpoise," which describes the shark's shape, and "beagle," which refers to its uncanny knack for hunting (just like the dog).

Big black eyes take in the surroundings.

The body is stout.

Skin is dark gray fading to a white underbelly.

Teeth are smooth and bladelike.

Pointy snout is useful for cutting through water.

VITAL STATS
Porbeagle Shark (Lamna nasus)

Length: 10 ft (3 m)
Weight: 500 lbs (227 kg)
Reproduction: ovoviviparous
Diet: small bony fish, cephalopods such as squid and octopus
Conservation status: critically endangered

FAKO MAKO

Porbeagles look so much like makos that they're often mistaken for the more desirable game fish. Fishermen have even dubbed porbeagles "fakos."

WARM-BODIED

Like other mackerel sharks, the warm-bodied porbeagle is ready to sprint. Having a body temperature warmer than the surrounding water keeps its muscles warm, which allows for great bursts of speed.

SANDTIGER SHARK

This shark is also called the ragged tooth shark (in South Africa) and the gray nurse shark (in Australia), although it's not related to nurse sharks.

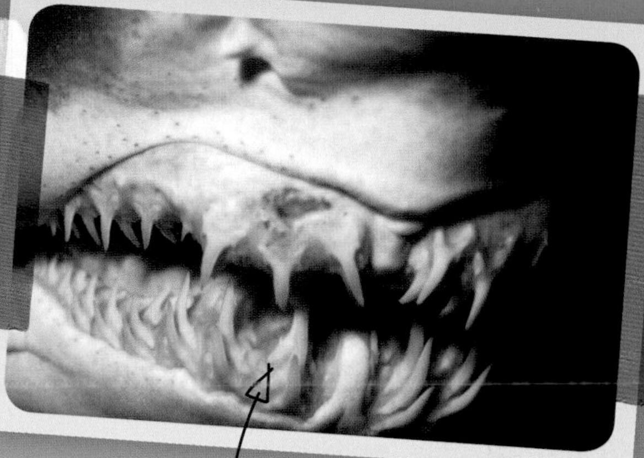

REAL WINDBAGS

Most sharks need to keep moving or else they'll sink. Sandtigers, however, have figured out a trick that lets them stay afloat while staying put: They come to the surface and gulp in air. They keep some of it in their stomachs and either burp or fart out the rest. They control the amount of air in their bellies and hover in the water where they want. No joke.

Crazy teeth jut out even when the mouth is closed.

Pointy snout is cone-shaped.

Two dorsal fins are similar in size.

Upper lobe of the caudal fin (tail) is much longer than lower.

Did you know?

Sandtiger sharks were nearly hunted to extinction in Australia. They are the first sharks to become a protected species, in 1984.

VITAL STATS
Sandtiger Shark (Carcharias taurus)

Length: 6 to 10 ft (2 to 3 m)

Weight: 200 to 350 lbs (90 to 160 kg)

Reproduction: ovoviviparous

Diet: bony fish, crustaceans, rays, squids, and other sharks

Conservation status: vulnerable

The Chondrichthyes Chronicles

"All the News That's Fit to Swim"

VOLUME I: EARLY EDITION

DATE: YESTERDAY

PRICE: 50 CLAMS

AUTHOR PUTS SOME TEETH INTO HIS TALE

Mako shark gives more than a mouthful

By Ernesto Waterway

Man versus nature is a tried-and-true literary theme. In Ernest Hemingway's acclaimed 1952 novel *The Old Man and the Sea*, nature takes the form of some hungry sea predators that go after an old man's impressive catch-of-the-day—a huge marlin that he hopes will net him a much-needed sum of money. During the course of one exhausting night, the fisherman battles a gigantic mako, as well as packs of other sharks.

Although the book is famed for its understanding of the sea and the respect it shows for the sharks, it isn't entirely accurate. The author took some literary license to juice up the story, and the behaviors he describes aren't quite true to nature. He also gave the mako eight rows of teeth, when in reality these fish have just two or three. That's still a lot of bite for your buck.

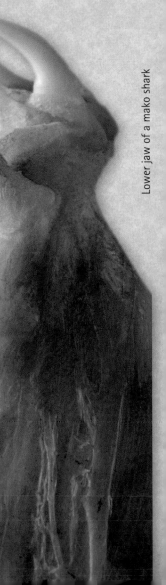

Lower jaw of a mako shark

Ernest Hemingway won the Pulitzer Prize in 1953, and the Nobel Prize for Literature in 1954.

CLUB MED OR CLUB DEAD?

Sharks could be swimming toward oblivion in the Mediterranean Sea

By SANDY TRAWLER

It appears that the sunny Mediterranean is one of the world's most dangerous places to be if you're a shark. According to the World Conservation Union, the waters between Europe and Africa have the highest percentage of shark and ray species currently at risk—a staggering 42 percent.

Bottom-dwellers are particularly vulnerable because of intensive seafloor fishing. The seabed-hugging Maltese skate, for instance, is critically endangered, with recent population declines estimated at 80 percent.

Two other imperiled species are the shortfin mako and the porbeagle shark, both critically endangered. Prized for their meat and fins, these sharks are being fished far faster than they reproduce.

The white shark also comes in as endangered, showing an alarming 50 to 60 percent drop in numbers in the region.

Of all the shark and ray species that call the Mediterranean home, 30 are threatened with extinction, 13 are critically endangered, 8 are endangered, 9 are vulnerable, and 10 are considered in the clear—for now.

So what are the culprits behind this population plummet? The usual suspects are to blame: habitat destruction, sport fishing, human interference in the forms of tourism and development, commercial overfishing, and declines in shark foodie favorites such as the bluefin tuna.

1,063-POUND, 12-FOOT 6-INCH MAKO HOOKED OFF FLORIDA COAST

Massive mako meets its end

By LINUS HOOK

Destin, Florida, April 2007—A 1,000-plus pound (454-plus kg) shortfin mako hooked near the Gulf of Mexico in Destin, Florida, almost made the record books. But not without putting up a good fight—the mako in question gave it her all, proving a worthy opponent. It took anglers on two boats—the *Sea Ya Later II* and the *Mother Lode*—to bring in the big fish.

After the shark died, it required eight men to pull her on board. She was just shy of the largest mako ever caught: a 1,221-pound (554-kg) male caught in Massachusetts in 2001. While these types of catches certainly bring glory to the fishermen, they are also of scientific use because they allow up-close study of large, dangerous species.

Beautiful makos

EL TORO

¡Olé! Perhaps you're ready for a little time with the bull shark. This barrel-chested shark is one of nature's most adaptable and fascinating predators.

The upper lobe of the tail is much longer than the lower and has a notch.

A formidable hunter, it regularly swims up freshwater rivers in search of prey. Because of its preference for murky shallows, the bull shark often comes into contact with humans, giving it a rep for being a man-eater.

RUNNING OF THE BULLS

This predator lives all around the world, in tropical and subtropical waters, near coastlines and the mouths of rivers. In fact, major rivers on almost every continent provide snacks and shelter to the bull shark, including the Ganges (India), the Zambezi (southern Africa), the Amazon (South America), the Brisbane (Australia), and even the mighty Mississippi. A bull shark was caught as far north as Lake Michigan off the coast of Chicago back in 1955!

It gets its name from its bull-like shape. Compared to other sharks of the same length, the bull is much thicker around the middle, giving it a stout appearance.

BULL FIGHTING

Because bull sharks live in shallow, murky water close to shore, run-ins with humans are bound to happen. Although humans are never on a shark's menu, a bull shark may be more likely than not to take a bite if it feels cornered by a person. In fact, some scientists believe that bull sharks pose a much greater risk to humans than white sharks or tiger sharks based on proximity alone.

UP THE RIVER

There is only a handful of animals that can tolerate—and thrive—in both saltwater and freshwater. The bull shark is one of them. This spectacular animal is known to swim thousands of miles upriver in search of prey, a technique it uses to its advantage. Instead of chasing lunch that can escape into the deep sea, the bull shark can snatch a meal in the relatively close quarters of a riverbed.

LONE BULL

Bull sharks are often solitary creatures that spend most of their lives traveling alone.

The jaw is set low and ends behind the eyes.

VITAL STATS
Bull Shark (Carcharhinus leucas)

Length: females up to 11.5 ft (3.5 m)

Weight: 300 lbs (136 kg); females larger than males

Reproduction: viviparous

Diet: fish, rays, crabs, seals, turtles, seabirds, and other sharks

NURSERY TIME

Bull sharks give birth to live young after a gestation of 10 to 11 months in the brackish—or salty—water of protected river estuaries. Litters usually contain up to 13 pups, which often have dark markings on their fins. As with all other shark species, mom doesn't hang around too long, leaving the newly born pups to fend for themselves. While adult bull sharks don't have any natural predators, the pups often fall victim to the hunger pangs of larger sharks—including adult bull sharks.

Did you know?

Scientists in Central America used to think that the sharks they found in Lake Nicaragua were a species unique to the lake. But then they realized that their finned friends were actually bull sharks that had jumped the rapids to get to the lake.

>>HUNTING TECHNIQUE

Despite their small, beady eyes, bull sharks have pretty good eyesight. They tend to use an "observe and bite" technique of hunting: They watch an object and take an exploratory bite to gauge tastiness. If the victim fights back, the strong, quick bull is more than up to the challenge, often overcoming its prey quickly and decisively.

Eyes are rather small.

Teeth are triangular and serrated.

CHOW DOWN

Hippos

Even pelicans make the menu.

Scallops

Octopus

BIG APPETITE

Much like the tiger shark, the bull shark will eat nearly anything it can swallow, including fish, sharks, mollusks, birds, mammals, and carcasses of dead animals. Everything from hippos to human hair have been found in the bellies of these beasts.

The Chondrichthyes Chronicles

"All the News That's Fit to Swim"

VOLUME I: EARLY EDITION

DATE: WINTER

PRICE: 50 CLAMS

SINK OR SWIM

Bull sharks sink shrimp boat in Florida

By Bubba Forrest

Fort Myers Beach, Florida—In January, 2007, a shrimp boat captain and crew had to abandon ship after a bull shark rammed their vessel.

As is common in shrimping, the sharks were following the boat and feasting on bycatch tossed overboard. The captain reported that this happens often, and that sharks swimming nearby and accidently bumping into a fishing boat is an everyday occurrence. But this trip was different.

After four days of the sharks being pushier than usual, one of the animals rammed the boat, damaging the engine. The boat started taking on water, and the captain radioed for help. Two hours later a partner boat picked up the men. They tried to tow the damaged boat into shore, but it eventually sank.

Editor's Note:
Florida sharks would like you to know that this was actually a rare occurrence, and that bull sharks don't often ram boats.

Shrimp boats, as shown above, tend to be rather large.

SHARK NAMES

Where did "requiem" come from anyway?

By Belle E. Upp

A requiem is a mass for the dead, or music sung at a funeral service. So why would scientists name this group of sharks—which includes the bull, tiger, lemon, blue, blacktip, and oceanic whitetip, among others—"requiem" sharks? There are many theories.

Sailors from long ago often said that if a comrade fell into the sea when these sharks were present, he'd never come back. This associated the sharks with death, hence "requiem."

Another story, however, says that requiem sharks got their name because sailors spotted them in fair weather, when the sea was calm. In this case requiem implies "rest."

A third theory is that requiem comes from the French, *requin*, which means "shark."

So which is it? Your guess is as good as mine.

The French call the bull shark *requin bouledogue* (bulldog shark).

A Bahamas-based bull shark

BULL SHARKS IN THE BAHAMAS: A DIFFERENT KIND OF FISH

By Bob Marlin

All shark species have certain personality traits. Some are active, others are shy; you get the idea. All of these labels, however, are generalizations, and there are always exceptions to the rule.

Bull sharks are considered to be one of the more aggressive species in the ocean. But travel to the Bahamas and you'll find a very different kind of bull shark. The bulls in the Bahamas are a calm, mellow bunch. They are content to swim in the clear blue water, feasting on the abundant fish and staying away from high-traffic swim areas. Seems the island life agrees with them.

TIGER SHARK

And here's another of the big three: the mighty tiger shark. With a rep as fierce as the big cat it's named for, the tiger shark is one of nature's most successful predators. Family traits are round eyes and long pectoral fins behind five gill slits. The biggest of the requiem bunch, the tiger is one of the world's most common sharks.

GLOBE-TROTTERS

Tiger sharks get around—they can travel 50 miles (80 km) a day at speeds of up to 20 mph (32 kph) on transoceanic voyages, although they don't travel this far very often. They're not social butterflies, either: They usually make the trek alone.

Tiger sharks may seem sluggish, but they get revved up once they spot a potential meal.

EXTENDED FAMILY

Tiger shark pups are born in the spring and summer, and hatch from eggs inside the mother's body. They're about 2 feet (61 cm) long at birth and can be one of 80 in a litter. With that many kids, do you think they have a problem with sibling rivalry?

NIGHT OWL?

The tiger likes shallow water, although sometimes it spends its days in deep water and moves nearer to shore at night.

Eyes are big and sight is sharp.

*Tiger, tiger burning bright
In the forests of the night,
What immortal hand or eye
could frame thy fearful
symmetry?*

English poet William Blake may have been writing about the land-based beast, but the words certainly fit when describing its sea-dwelling namesake.

The teeth are serrated, like a steak knife.

Under the shark dental plan, when a front tooth wears out, a spare moves in from behind to replace it.

VITAL STATS
Tiger Shark (Galeocerdo cuvier)

Length: up to 18 ft (5.5 m)

Weight: 1,300 lbs (590 kg)

Reproduction: ovoviviparous

Diet: fish, sea turtles, seals, and just about anything else it can sink its teeth into

CHOW DOWN

Sea turtles are delicious.

This shark didn't feel so well . . .

SEASICK

When a tiger shark eats something it can't stomach, it simply vomits everything up by flipping its stomach out of its mouth. Now that's some serious indigestion!

Ready for a drumroll? One tiger was found with a 13.5-lb (6-kg) tom-tom drum in its stomach.

NOT-SO-PICKY-PALATE

Everything but the kitchen sink (and even that's negotiable)—that would pretty much sum up what the tiger shark will eat. It is one of the few species of shark that is a true scavenger. While it prefers fish, shellfish, turtles, squid, and the like, it will try just about anything, including garbage. Items found in the bellies of these beasts include tin cans, tires, beer bottles, bags of potatoes, coal, dogs, overcoats, license plates, a cow's hoof, deer antlers, undigested lobsters, and a chicken coop and feathers.

Seals are on the menu.

NEW YORK
DMD 239

CHOW DOWN

License plates are crunchy.

UNIQUE SHARK

Tiger sharks are the only ovoviviparous requiem sharks. All other requiems are viviparous.

"I think I'll have a little snack."

Caught as bycatch, this poor shark loses its fin.

IN THE SOUP

Fished for its valuable fins, which are used in soups and folk remedies, the tiger shark is under threat in some parts of the world. The barbaric practice of finning is outlawed in countries worldwide, but the law isn't always enforced.

CONSERVATION ALERT

Sensors running down the sides of the tiger shark's body sense movement in the water, giving the tiger shark a hunting edge.

The dark stripes that give the shark its name get lighter with age.

The spiracle near the shark's eye is a rudimentary gill slit.

>>RUNNER-UP

The white shark may have the fiercest rep, but tiger sharks finish a close second when it comes to the number of injuries to humans. That's not, however, because humans are their favorite fare. It's most likely because these big sharks swim close to shore—and so do we—and because they're not the most discerning diners. They'll try to eat anything when they are hungry. And that includes people.

The Chondrichthyes Chronicles

"All the News That's Fit to Swim"

VOLUME I: EARLY EDITION

DATE: JUNE

PRICE: 50 CLAMS

LONG ARM OF THE LAW

Australian gangster James Smith's arm winds up as fish food

By Oz Bait

Sydney, Australia, 1935—Tiger sharks are notorious for their ability to eat just about anything. But did you know they've also been instrumental in solving murders?

This enormous tiger shark was caught in 1949.

Back in April 1935, father-and-son operators of the Sydney Aquarium have a lucky day fishing when they catch a large tiger shark. Knowing it will be a big hit with visitors, the catch-

of-the-day is promptly put on display. Unfortunately, the shark is feeling a bit out of sorts. In the middle of an exhibition it shocks onlookers by vomiting up a man's tattooed arm, providing more of a show than anyone had bargained for.

Upon closer inspection, it becomes clear that the arm wasn't bitten off of its original owner, but rather hacked off with a knife, and not by a surgeon. A murder investigation is soon underway, the press is having a field day, and the city finds itself in the grips of a "murder most foul."

The mystery arm—with some distinctive tattoos—is eventually identified as that of a small-time Australian gangster named James Smith. After a few coincidences and some twists and turns, one of Smith's crooked mates 'fesses up to the crime, admitting that he killed Smith, cut him up, and threw the arm into the water because it wouldn't fit with the rest of Smith's body. Case closed.

ART IMITATES SHARK

Just when you thought it was safe to go back into . . . the museum?

By Ray Gills

New York City, 2007—Majestic sea creatures they may be, but who knew that sharks could make such a big splash in the world of art? British artist Damien Hirst, that's who. One of a group of artists dubbed the YBAs (Young British Artists), Hirst was commissioned by world-famous art collector Charles Saatchi in 1991 to create whatever art his heart desired. For Hirst, that art necessitated . . . a shark. So the artist hired an Australian fisherman to snag him one, with the specific instruction that it be "something big enough to eat you."

To the tune of £50,000 ($75,000), Hirst used the animal to create *The Physical Impossibility of Death in the Mind of Someone Living*, which featured a 14-foot (4-m) tiger shark suspended in formaldehyde within a glass tank. First exhibited in London in 1992, the shark was referred to in the British press as "a £50,000 fish without chips."

Damien Hirst and his shark

Seems that artist knew best: The work was nominated for the Turner Prize (which you artsy types know is a big deal) and in 2004 sold for $8 million, the second-highest price ever paid for a living artist's work. This famous tiger has been displayed in large museums around the world (although the current shark is a replacement of the original, which had started to rot).

SMART LIKE A SHARK

Captive tiger shark proves to be a real smarty-pants

By Michael J. Tilapia

Cook Islands, New Zealand, 1983—Famous shark filmmaker Valerie Taylor learned firsthand just how clever sharks can be, which is not surprising, considering that pound-for-pound they have a lot of brain for fish.

In 1983, Taylor was filming a captive male tiger shark—all 12 feet (3.6 m) of him. As would be expected, he swam at a steady pace around the enclosure of his pen. Just after he had passed Taylor on his leisurely stroll, she noticed a small fish that was trying to squeeze through some wire mesh in the pen. Feeling kindly, she made a small opening to set the fish free, and sure as can be, the shark suddenly appeared on the scene. He, too, tried to help the fish by pushing his blunt snout into the gap, bracing against the bottom, and pushing against the barrier in an attempt to lift it. After a few failed attempts, the shark gave up and continued quietly on his way.

Though often pegged as "brainless" hunters, sharks can learn and remember as well as many mammals. In fact, tiger sharks are known to improve their hunting techniques by trial and error. Maybe they know as we do: Nothing ventured, nothing gained.

GREAT WHITE

And here we are . . . seeking out the most famous of sharks: the great white. These days it mostly goes by the name white shark, but through the years it's also been known as the white pointer, white death, and great white. Start putting the shark cage together, as free swimming with these sharks is just plain crazy.

OCEAN ROAMERS

Whites are social sharks which spend much of their time in shallow temperate waters. They're also known to make long treks across the ocean, probably in search of prey and mates.

The top and bottom of the tail are about the same size, which is characteristic of mackerel sharks.

TAG, YOU'RE IT!

Despite being the most famous of all the sharks, whites are actually a rare species, about which we know very little. Tagging programs around the world are trying to change that. Research vessels (much like the *Lucky Chum*) bait and immobilize sharks so that they can attach radio-transmitting tags to their dorsal fins. These tags don't hurt the shark or slow it down. But they do supply information about where the sharks swim and how deep they dive.

Large, black eyes do not have nictitating membranes. During feeding the shark's eyes roll back into its head for protection.

White sharks have triangular serrated teeth.

VITAL STATS
White Shark (Carcharodon carcharias)

Length: 13 to 16 ft (4 to 5 m)

Weight: more than 1,500 to 2,400 lbs (680 to 1,089 kg)

Reproduction: viviparous

Diet: marine mammals, fish, sharks, sea turtles

Conservation status: vulnerable

The jaw is set low and far back, but extends forward when the shark is grabbing prey.

The white shark is only white on its belly. The top of its body is gray to almost black.

WHITE SHARK CAFÉ

White sharks who live along the west coast of North America have been making winter pilgrimages to a remote area of the Pacific between Hawaii and Baja California dubbed the white shark café. The sharks who travel there tend to loiter for weeks and often dive deeper than 1,000 feet (305 m) multiple times a day. Despite the name, scientists think the sharks are there for mating purposes, not for food.

DENTAL DIVA

While many shark species have serrated teeth, none are quite as efficient as the white shark's. The choppers in this shark's mouth are huge, flat triangles with incredibly sharp serrations running down each side. After the powerful jaws have clamped down, all a white shark has to do is move its head and the teeth slice through prey like a hot knife through butter.

Superteeth in action!

Seals are nice and blubbery.

CHOW DOWN

So are sea lions.

BAD MANNERS

White sharks in South Africa's False Bay are known to hurl themselves out of the water while seal hunting. Some have been observed tossing the seals high in the air before devouring them. Don't they know it's rude to play with your food?

>>ROCKET TO STARDOM

While white sharks have always fascinated and frightened, many believe that their terrifying reputation really took off after the 1975 movie *Jaws*, which was based on Peter Benchley's novel about a man-eating shark.

Did you know?
The largest white shark ever caught was a female measuring 21 feet (6.4 m) and weighing a whopping 7,300 lbs (3,311 kg)! She was caught in 1945 off the coast of Cuba.

MMMM . . . PEOPLE . . .

Do white sharks really enjoy the taste of humans? Absolutely not. For starters, we don't have nearly enough fat for them. No, we're definitely not the catch of the day for these apex predators.

So what do white sharks choose from the great buffet of the deep? Anything that will provide lots of energy (which usually means blubber): seals, sea lions, large fish (like tuna), sharks, and sea turtles.

Did you know?
Of the 80 to 90 humans hurt by sharks each year worldwide, fewer than 6 are harmed by white sharks.

MAGNIFICENT LIVING SCULPTURE

Human fascination with white sharks stems from the power, size, and apparent ferocity of these animals. In reality, they're simply big fish doing what big fish do: swimming, eating, having babies, and swimming some more. They're no more aggressive than any other large predator in the sea.

White sharks head to the shallows to hunt.

Cage divers lay bait to attract white sharks. Some worry that the sharks will start to associate cages with an easy meal.

ROOMMATE RAGE

Female white shark fatally bites two tank mates at Monterey Bay Aquarium

BY FIONA FINN

Monterey, California, March 2005—A young female white shark has killed two soupfin sharks (or tope sharks) with which she shared a tank. The two separate attacks occurred only weeks apart, and have shaken the aquarium staff and angered critics.

The white shark was brought to the aquarium in September 2004, after being caught accidentally by a halibut fisherman. Local biologists did not expect her to live very long, as previous attempts at keeping a white shark in captivity lasted no longer than 16 days. But this feisty female has been at the aquarium for six months.

The biting incidents have incensed critics who believe that such a large predatory fish should not be kept in captivity under any circumstances. And while the aquarium has always planned to return the shark to her natural habitat, aquarium staff are getting concerned that she may soon grow too large to transfer safely back to the open ocean. Still, they are enjoying the thrill of having her around.

The record for keeping a white shark in captivity remains 198 days.

Editor's note:

After 198 days in captivity, the white shark was released back into the wild with a tracking device. Biologists hope to keep tabs on her for some time to get valuable information about her travels, habits, and health.

NICOLE KIDMAN A MARATHONER?

Shark named Nicole makes marathon journey across Indian Ocean

By SPEEDY BULLER

In 2003, researcher Ramón Bonfil of the Wildlife Conservation Society tagged a large female white shark off the coast of South Africa. Her tag popped off a few months later, near the coast of Australia. The shark had traveled across the entire Indian Ocean in a matter of months!

Then, a few months after that, Bonfil and his associates spotted the same shark back in South Africa.

"There's absolutely no doubt it's the same shark," Bonfil said. "It's identifiable by the notches on its fin. It's like a fingerprint." Nicknamed Nicole (after Australian actress Nicole Kidman), the shark had traveled from South Africa to Australia and back again in nine months. No shark on record has ever traveled that far—more than 6,800 miles (almost 11,000 km)—so quickly.

Why'd she go? Bonfil believes it was for mating purposes, although nobody is sure. Some scientists believe these long treks could be normal behavior for white sharks. In 2002, a tagged white shark swam from California to Hawaii and back, a distance greater than 5,000 miles (8,050 km). Although not as fast as Nicole, that shark's journey suggests that no matter where they live on the planet, white sharks may have some impressive species-specific behavior.

SHARK JUMPING TIPS FROM THE EXPERTS

Listen up all white sharks! Ever since we showed the humans how high we can jump, they've been coming to the False Bay/Seal Island corridor in droves to watch us. Want to impress?

JOIN OUR THREE-DAY WORKSHOP!

DAY 1: Seal-spotting techniques and hunting lectures. Find out how to avoid the dreaded seal-or-surfer mistake, and discover why hunting at dawn and dusk are still your best bets.

DAY 2: Acceleration tips for the most effective—and impressive—surface-breaking moments and in-air flair. (Hint: Start deep, swim hard, think perpendicular, and POW!)

DAY 3: Small-group work to perfect your landings. Going for a big splash or a dramatic twist of your tail? We'll show you how.

PAYMENT is a swim in the park: Simply arrive each morning with a small to mid-sized seal or large bony fish. We also accept American Express.

NOTE: Workshops can be arduous. It's always advisable to discuss any new workout plan with your doctor.

WANT TO GET MORE
HEIGHT?

WANT MORE
SEAL SNACKS
GUARANTEED?

WANT TO ADD MORE FLAIR
TO YOUR **LANDINGS?**

They call it "breaching," we call it "flying"!

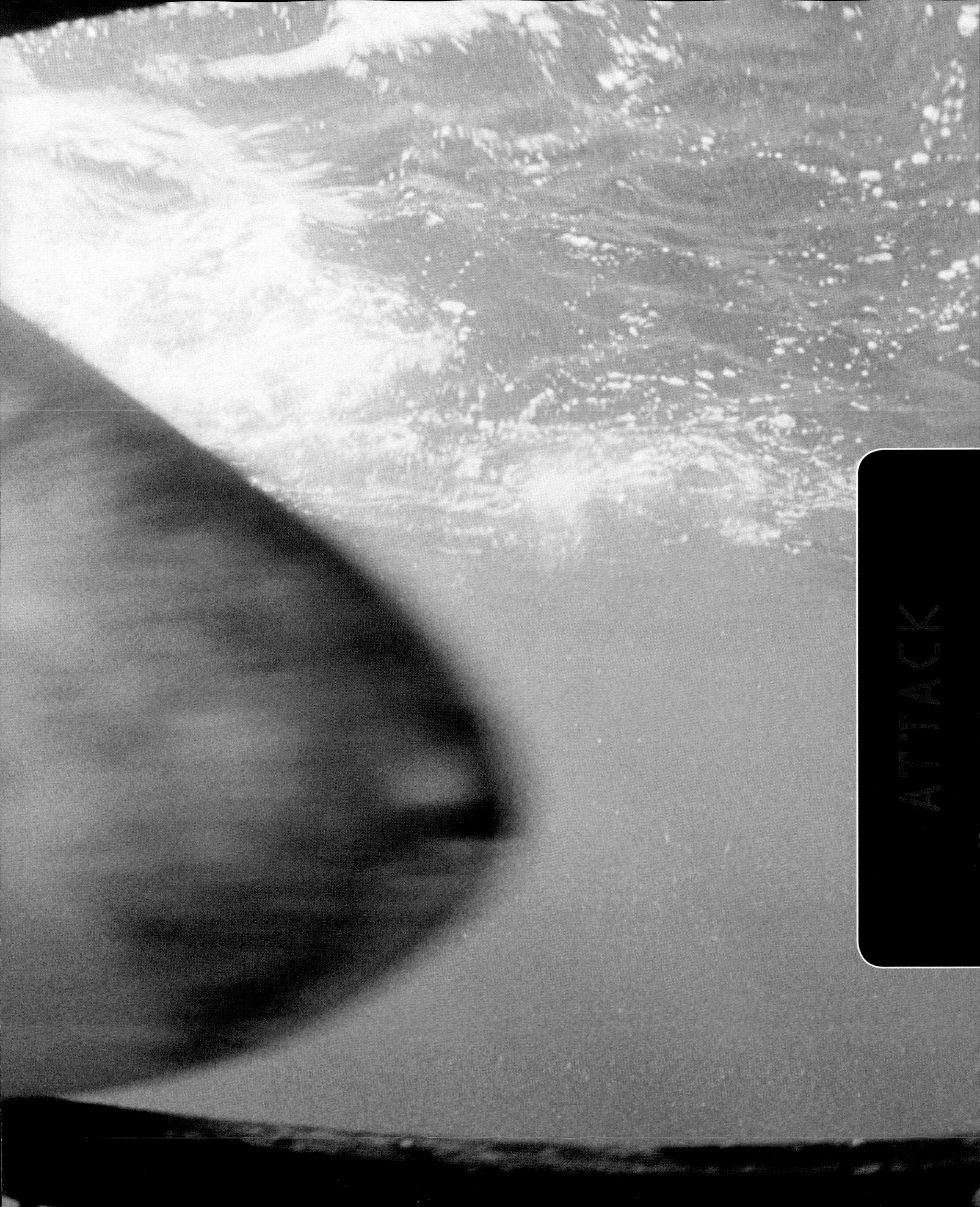

Shark Attack!

Each year anywhere from 50 to 100 people worldwide are bitten by sharks. About eight of them die. Regardless, most people who swim or dive in the ocean list "shark attack" as one of their greatest fears.

Is that fair to our finned friends? Not really. While it's smart to be aware of your surroundings and the likelihood of a shark being nearby, it's also good to keep your fears in perspective.

EACH YEAR YOU'RE MORE LIKELY TO BE BITTEN BY THE FOLLOWING CREATURES THAN BY A SHARK:

- Bees
- Wasps
- Scorpions
- Spiders
- Snakes
- Cats
- Dogs
- Pigs
- Humans

A shark cage allows people to get close, but keeps sharks and divers safe.

1916: A BAD YEAR FOR SHARKS

Author Peter Benchley got his idea for *Jaws* from a series of shark attacks off the New Jersey shore in 1916. Between July 1 and July 12, five people were bitten by sharks, and four of them died. Very little was known about sharks at that time, and the media had a field day. Sharks were sensationalized and vilified around the country. A small white shark with human remains in its gut was caught on July 14, but chances are that more than one shark was responsible. Three of the attacks took place in a brackish creek 16 miles (25.7 km) inland from the ocean—the domain of a bull shark, not a white. To this day, scientists can't agree on the culprit(s)—or cause—of the attacks.

CONSIDER THIS

While an average of eight people die each year at the hand of sharks, thirty to one hundred million sharks die each year at the hands of humans. We are a much bigger threat to them than they are to us.

I know what you're thinking: If it's so unlikely that a shark is going to bite me, then why does it happen at all? Well, sharks are animals, and they're hardwired to behave certain ways and learn by exploring their world just like you do. And in our increasingly small world, sometimes sharks find themselves up close and personal with unfamiliar creatures (including humans), which is when a bite may happen.

Teen surfer Bethany Hamilton lost her arm to a shark off the coast of Hawaii in 2003. She's still surfs, and well!

SHARK BITES

The most common reason for a shark to bite a human is curiosity. Sharks learn by exploring their environment, and since they don't have hands, they explore with their (toothy) mouths. When humans splash they may seem like wounded fish. If humans are swimming in an area where fish are caught, they may smell like fish (at least to a shark). A nearby shark might slowly come closer to investigate. This slow approach often gives people time to leave the water, or results in a superficial bite.

Larger, more damaging bites occur when a shark feels challenged or threatened. This can happen in a number of ways: A shark may feel as if it is competing for food when it grabs a fish speared by a fisherman. A shark may feel cornered if a swimmer unwittingly blocks it from open water. A shark may feel threatened when it is touched, hooked, speared, or finned. All of these scenarios (called "provoked attacks") put a shark on the defensive, and its natural instincts kick in. The shark does not know that human skin is fragile, and so it bites with the same intensity as it bites any other competitor.

So now we understand a shark's motivation. But why are some bites superficial and others lethal? That depends on a host of factors: How far from shore is the bite victim? Are there people around to help? Did the shark bite once or multiple times? What part of the body has been hurt? All of these factors play a role in the health and survival of the victim. Most deaths occur because the victim bleeds to death before help arrives, not because a shark has been particularly vicious.

So when you're in the ocean, remember that you're on the shark's turf. Respect its habitat and be aware of your surroundings. If you forget that, trouble may follow!

While chain mail can protect from cuts, it can't protect from the crushing power of a shark's jaws.

THE BIG THREE

While all large sharks are potentially dangerous to humans, three are considered the most dangerous: the white, tiger, and bull. This is because these three are very large, they hunt animals that are about the same size as we are, and they swim in the areas in which we swim.

Rodney Fox was bitten by a white shark in 1963. He has since become an expert on the species.

Keep your arms and legs inside the cage at all times!

Caution! Even this little guy could do some damage.

EVEN THOUGH I'VE BEEN DRILLING IT INTO YOUR HEAD THAT YOUR CHANCES OF COMING FACE-TO-FACE WITH A SHARK ARE SUPER SLIM, THERE ARE DEFINITELY WAYS TO FURTHER ENSURE YOUR SAFETY WHEN SWIMMING, SNORKELING, AND DIVING:

- This one is obvious: Do NOT go swimming if large sharks are present! If you're swimming and spot a big shark, then quickly and calmly leave the water.
- Do not harass or touch any shark, even a small one. Any shark is capable of inflicting injury.
- Do not corner a shark, or cut off its path to open water. It may feel threatened and act defensively.
- Be aware of your surroundings and the marine life nearby. Their behavior may alert you to the presence of large predators (i.e. sharks).
- Keep your splashing and erratic movements to a minimum, as they can mimic those of an injured animal and attract the attention of a shark.
- Don't go swimming at dawn or dusk, as that's when many species of shark hunt.
- Don't swim too far from shore, as you'll be farther from help should you need it.

- Never swim, surf, or dive alone.
- Be very careful when swimming between sandbars or near steep drop-offs. Sharks hunt there.
- If groups of small fish are leaping at the surface (or above it), leave the water immediately. It means that predators, possibly sharks, are feeding on the fish.
- Don't wear shiny jewelry, as it can reflect light much the way fish scales do. And what do sharks like to eat? Fish!
- Don't wear high-contrast bathing suits, as sharks can see contrast very well. Even an uneven sunburn can be spotted by a shark.
- Don't swim in murky water, or water with garbage or animal waste, as sharks will be attracted to the smell. That said, you shouldn't be swimming in dirty water anyway. Gross.

OKAY, SO DESPITE ALL THE PRECAUTIONS, YOU FIND YOURSELF IN THE CROSSHAIRS OF A SHARK'S RADAR. WHAT DO YOU DO? DON'T PANIC. EASIER SAID THAN DONE, I KNOW. BUT TRY.

IF YOU'RE SWIMMING:

- Get out of the water as quickly as you can.
- Keep your movements as crisp and smooth as possible. Screaming and flailing will only entice the shark to come closer.
- If you're swimming in a group, get everyone to kick together in even strokes.
- If the shark brushes or bumps you, keep heading toward shore as quickly as you can.
- If the shark gets you in its mouth, fight like mad. Punch, kick, whack whatever you can. Go for its sensitive spots, especially the eyes and gills.
- Get out of the water as quickly as you can!

IF YOU'RE SCUBA DIVING:

- Stay calm and still. Chances are the shark is just curious and will swim right by.
- If you've been spearfishing or collecting mollusks, drop them and calmly swim away. Cut your losses and let the shark have your snack.
- If the shark isn't losing interest, then get out of the water as calmly and quickly as you can, never letting the shark out of your sight.
- If the shark actually starts to lunge at you, back up against any available outcropping or reef. This will make it hard for the shark to get a grip on you.
- Use anything possible to fend off the shark: stick, spear, camera, shells, rocks, anything.
- Hit the shark on the nose. They don't like this, and will often retreat after a good whack. They might come back, so get away quickly whenever you can.
- If the shark gets you in its mouth, fight like mad. Punch, kick, whack whatever you can. Go for its sensitive spots, especially the eyes and gills.
- Get out of the water as quickly as you can.

Could you keep your cool if this were you?

SCIENCE TO THE RESCUE!

Scientists around the world are constantly developing new ways to protect swimmers. Many beaches in Australia and South Africa use huge nets to keep large, curious animals away from humans. While they can be effective, these nets are by no means foolproof. They're also controversial, as animals can get stuck in them and drown.

Some scientists are investigating the usefulness of electric shock barriers, which pulse electric current in the water to keep sharks at bay. The problem with this, however, is that beachgoers get shocked, too. Other scientists are developing shark repellent chemicals that can be shot by air cannon (say, from a lifeguard tower) into the water to keep sharks away from swimmers.

The effectiveness of these myriad methods are questionable at this point, but technology and science move forward by leaps and bounds every day. Many believe that we're on the cusp of finding safe, effective ways to keep both sharks and people safe.

Attack Map

While humans and sharks don't come into contact with one another all that often, it does happen (as we have just discussed). Scientists and governments (not to mention swimmers, surfers, divers, and fishermen) like to keep tabs on our toothy compadres, and to track where and when bites occur. This map shows worldwide hot spots.

TOTAL BITES IN THE LAST 400 YEARS (OR SO):

- Mainland USA (mostly Florida): 880
- Hawaii: 113
- Central America: 61
- Caribbean: 65
- South America (mostly Brazil): 100
- Europe: 39
- Africa (mostly South Africa): 276
- Asia: 117
- Pacific Islands: 131
- Australia (mostly New South Wales): 345
- New Zealand: 47

As you might guess (having read this mighty tome), the areas that have the most recorded bites share two very important factors: large sharks live nearby, and so do large populations of beach-going humans. What the numbers listed above do not show, however, is that as we have learned more about sharks and their behavior, and as technology has improved, the rate of attacks per year is on the decline. This is very good news for all species.

If you find yourself visiting the ruins of the *Titanic*, you won't have to worry about shark attacks—the icy cold temperatures are far more fatal this close to the Arctic!

Up here, the coast is clear. Literally. So It's a great place to take your shark-fearing grandmother, but make sure she knits you both super-warm sweaters first.

The bull sharks that swim up the Amazon River tend to head deep inland to Peru. So if you're swimming in the Amazon, stay in Brazil!

If you choose to bathe off the coast of New South Wales, heed my safety advice—or consider a steel swimsuit.

Considering a Pacific Island vacation? Go for it, but these lovely, sunny islands have some dark, murky waters. Remember what that means!

shark superlatives

What shark book would be complete without the list of biggest, baddest, fastest, maddest? Well, here's ours.

I have to say, though, that research and technology have made these lists very difficult to maintain. New, incredible shark info is discovered every day! So enjoy these incredible records, and let us know if you hear of any that have been beat. Thanks!

SMALLEST
DWARF LANTERNSHARK
(Etmopterus perryi):
topping out at 8 inches (21 cm)

LARGEST
WHALE SHARK *(Rhincodon typus):*
41.5 feet (12.6 m)
(This is the largest one ever caught. Reports of whale sharks exceeding 59 feet (18 m) have been recorded.)

LONGEST GESTATION
FRILLED SHARK
(Chlamydoselachus anguineus):
3.5 years

SHORTEST GESTATION
GREY BAMBOOSHARK
(Chiloscyllium griseum):
less than 80 days

The masterful mako holds the record for fastest shark.

FASTEST
SHORTFIN MAKO

(Isurus oxyrhincus):

clocked at more than 35 mph (56 kph)

MOST ABUNDANT SHARK
PIKED DOGFISH

(Squalus acanthias)

DEEPEST A SHARK HAS BEEN FOUND
PORTUGUESE DOGFISH

(Centroscymnus coelolepis):

12,060 feet (3,675 m)

MOST WIDELY TRAVELED SHARK
WHITE SHARK

(Carcharodon carcharias):

more than 6,800 miles
(almost 11,000 km)

BIGGEST EYES
BIGEYE THRESHER

(Alopias supercillosus):

larger than 4 inches (10 cm)
in diameter

STRONGEST BITE EVER RECORDED
DUSKY SHARK

(Carcharhinus obscurus):

132 lbs (60 kg) of force

(Many scientists believe that a white shark may very well exceed that.)

SMOOTHEST SKIN
SILKY SHARK

(Carcharhinus falciformis)

ROUGHEST SKIN
BRAMBLE SHARK

(Echinorhinus brucus)

LIST OF SPECIES

ORDER: HEXANCHIFORMES: Sixgill, Sevengill and Frilled Sharks
Family CHLAMYDOSELA: Frilled Sharks
Chlamydoselachus anguineus – Frilled shark
Chlamydoselachus sp. A – Southern African Frilled Shark

Family HEXANCHIDAE: Sixgill and Sevengill Sharks
Heptranchias perlo – Sharpnose sevengill shark
Hexanchus griseus – Bluntnose sixgill shark
Hexanchus nakamurai – Bigeye sixgill shark
Notorynchus cepedianus – Broadnose sevengill shark

ORDER: SQUALIFORMES: Dogfish Sharks
Family ECHINORHINIDAE: Bramble Sharks
Echinorhinus brucus – Bramble shark
Echinorhinus cookei – Prickly shark

Family SQUALIDAE - Dogfish sharks
Cirrhigaleus asper – Roughskin spurdog
Cirrhigaleus barbifer – Mandarin dogfish
Squalus acanthias – Piked dogfish
Squalus blainvillei – Longnose spurdog
Squalus cubensis – Cuban dogfish
Squalus japonicus – Japanese spurdog
Squalus megalops – Shortnose spurdog
Squalus melanurus – Blacktail spurdog
Squalus mitsukurii – Shortspine spurdog
Squalus rancureli – Cyrano spurdog
Squalus sp. A – Bartail Spurdog
Squalus sp. B – Eastern highfin spurdog
Squalus sp. C – Western highfin spurdog
Squalus sp. D – Fatspine spurdog
Squalus sp. E – Western longnose spurdog
Squalus sp. F – Eastern longnose spurdog

Family CENTROPHORIDAE – Gulper sharks
Centrophorus atromarginatus – Dwarf gulper shark
Centrophorus acus – Needle dogfish
Centrophorus granulosus – Gulper shark
Centrophorus harrissoni – Longnose gulper shark
Centrophorus isodon – Blackfin gulper shark
Centrophorus lusitanicus – Lowfin gulper shark
Centrophorus moluccensis – Smallfin gulper shark
Centrophorus niaukang – Taiwan gulper shark
Centrophorus squamosus – Leafscale gulper shark
Centrophorus tessellatus – Mosaic gulper shark
Deania calcea – Birdbeak dogfish
Deania hystricosum – Rough longnose dogfish
Deania profundorum – Arrowhead dogfish
Deania quadrispinosum – Longsnout dogfish

Family ETMOPTERIDAE – Lantern sharks
Aculeola nigra – Hooktooth dogfish
Centroscyllium excelsum – Highfin dogfish
Centroscyllium fabricii – Black dogfish
Centroscyllium granulatum – Granular dogfish
Centroscyllium kamoharai – Bareskin dogfish
Centroscyllium nigrum – Combtooth dogfish
Centroscyllium ornatum – Ornate dogfish
Centroscyllium ritteri – Whitefin dogfish
Etmopterus baxteri – Giant lanternshark
Etmopterus bigelowi – Blurred smooth lanternshark
Etmopterus brachyurus – Shorttail lanternshark
Etmopterus bullisi – Lined lanternshark
Etmopterus carteri – Cylindrical lanternshark
Etmopterus caudistigmus – Tailspot lanternshark
Etmopterus decacuspidatus – Combtooth lanternshark
Etmopterus dianthus – Pink lanternshark
Etmopterus dislineatus – Lined lanternshark
Etmopterus evansi – Blackmouth lanternshark
Etmopterus fusus – Pygmy lanternshark
Etmopterus gracilispinis – Broadband lanternshark
Etmopterus granulosus – Southern lanternshark
Etmopterus hillianus – Carribean lanternshark
Etmopterus litvinovi – Smalleye lanternshark
Etmopterus lucifer – Blackbelly lanternshark
Etmopterus molleri – Slendertail lanternshark
Etmopterus perryi – Dwarf lanternshark
Etmopterus polli – African lanternshark
Etmopterus princeps – Great lanternshark
Etmopterus pseudosqualiolus – False pygmy lanternshark
Etmopterus pusillus – Smooth lanternshark
Etmopterus pycnolepis – Densecale lanternshark
Etmopterus robinsi – West Indian lanternshark
Etmopterus schultzi – Fringefin lanternshark
Etmopterus sentosus – Thorny lanternshark

Etmopterus spinax – Velvet belly
Etmopterus splendidus – Splendid lanternshark
Etmopterus unicolor – Brown lanternshark
Etmopterus villosus – Hawaiian lanternshark
Etmopterus virens – Green lanternshark
Miroscyllium sheikoi – Rasptooth dogfish
Trigonognathus kabeyai – Viper dogfish

Family SOMNIOSIDAE – Sleeper sharks
Centroscymnus coelolepis – Portuguese dogfish
Centroscymnus owstoni – Roughskin dogfish
Centroselachus crepidater – Longnose velvet dogfish
Proscymnodon macracanthus – Largespine velvet dogfish
Proscymnodon plunketi – Plunket shark
Scymnodalatias albicanda – Whitetail dogfish
Scymnodalatias garricki – Azores dogfish
Scymnodalatias oligodon – Sparsetooth dogfish
Scymnodalatias sherwoodi – Sherwood dogfish
Scymnodon ringens – Knifetooth dogfish
Somniosus antarcticus – Southern sleeper shark
Somniosus longus – Frog shark
Somniosus microcephalus – Greenland shark
Somniosus pacificus – Pacific sleeper shark
Somniosus rostratus – Little sleeper shark
Zameus ichiharai – Japanese velvet dogfish
Zameus squamulosus – Velvet dogfish

Family OXYNOTIDAE – Roughsharks
Oxynotus bruniensis – Prickly dogfish
Oxynotus carribaeus – Carribean roughshark
Oxynotus centrina – Angular roughshark
Oxynotus japonicus – Japanese roughshark
Oxynotus paradoxus – Sailfin roughshark

Family DALATIIDAE – Kitefin sharks
Dalatias licha – Kitefin shark
Euprotomicroides zantedeschia – Taillight shark
Europtomicrus bispinatus – Pygmy shark
Heteroscymnoides marleyi – Longnose pygmy shark
Istius brasiliensis – Cookiecutter or cigar shark
Isistius labiali – South China cookiecutter shark
Isistius plutodus – Largetooth cookiecutter shark
Mollisquama parini – Pocket dogfish
Squaliolus aliae – Smalleye pygmy shark
Squaliolus laticaudus – Spined pygmy shark

ORDER: PRISTIOPHORIFORMES: Sawsharks
Family PRISTIOPHORIDAE – Sawsharks
Pliotrema warreni – Sixgill sawshark
Pristiophorus cirratus – Longnose sawshark
Pristiophorus japonicus – Japanese sawshark
Pristiophorus nudipinnis – Shortnose sawshark
Pristiophorus schroederi – Bahamas sawshark
Pristiophorus sp. A – Eastern sawshark
Pristiophorus sp. B – Tropical sawshark
Pristiophorus sp. C – Philippine sawshark
Pristiophorus sp. D – Dwarf sawshark

ORDER: SQUATINIFORMES: Angel Sharks
Family SQUATINIDAE – Angel Sharks
Squatina aculeata – Sawback angelshark
Squatina africana – African angelshark
Squatina argentina – Argentine angelshark
Squatina armata – Chilean angelshark
Squatina australis – Australian angelshark
Squatina californica – Pacific angelshark
Squatina dumeril – Sanddevil
Squatina formosa – Taiwan angelshark
Squatina guggenheim – Hidden angelshark
Squatina japonica – Japanese angelshark
Squatina nebulosa – Clouded angelshark
Squatina oculata – Smoothback angelshark
Squatina punctata – Angular angelshark
Squatina squatina – Angelshark
Squatina tergocellata – Ornate angelshark
Squatina tergocellatoides – Ocellated angelshark
Squatina sp. A – Eastern angelshark
Squatina sp. B – Western angelshark

ORDER: HETERODONTIFORMES: Bullhead Sharks
Family HETERODONTIDAE – Bullhead sharks
Heterodontus francisci – Horn shark
Heterodontus galeatus – Crested bullhead shark
Heterodontus japonicus – Japanese bullhead shark
Heterodontus mexicanus – Mexican hornshark
Heterodontus portusjacksoni – Port Jackson shark
Heterodontus quoyi – Galapagos bullhead shark
Heterodontus ramalheira – Whitespotted bullhead shark
Heterodontus zebra – Zebra bullhead shark

Heterodontus sp. A – Oman bullhead shark

ORDER: ORECTOLOBIFORMES: Carpet Sharks
Family PARASCYLLIIDAE – Collared Carpetsharks
Cirrhoscyllium expolitum – Barbelthroat carpetshark
Cirrhoscyllium formosanum – Taiwan saddled carpetshark
Cirrhoscyllium japonicum – Saddled carpetshark
Parascyllium collare – Collared carpetshark
Parascyllium ferrugineum – Rusty carpetshark
Parascyllium sparsimaculatum – Ginger carpetshark
Parascyllium variolatum – Necklace carpetshark or Varied carpetshark

Family BRACHAELURIDAE – Blind sharks
Brachaelurus waddi – Blind shark
Heteroscyllium colcloughi – Bluegrey carpetshark

Family ORECTOLOBIDAE – Wobbegongs
Eucrossorhinus dasypogon – Tasselled wobbegong
Orectolobus japonicus – Japanese wobbegong
Orectolobus maculatus – Spotted wobbegong
Orectolobus ornatus – Ornate wobbegong
Orectolobus wardi – Northern wobbegong
Orectolobus sp. A – Western wobbegong
Sutorectus tentaculatus – Cobbler wobbegong

Family HEMISCYLLIIDAE – Longtailed Carpetshark
Chiloscyllium arabicum – Arabian carpetshark
Chiloscyllium burmensis – Burmese bambooshark
Chiloscyllium griseum – Grey bambooshark
Chiloscyllium hasselti – Indonesian bambooshark
Chiloscyllium indicum – Slender bambooshark
Chiloscyllium plagiosum – Whitespotted bambooshark
Chiloscyllium punctatum – Brownbanded bambooshark
Hemiscyllium freycineti – Indonesian speckled carpetshark
Hemiscyllium hallstromi – Papuan epaulette shark
Hemiscyllium ocellatum – Epaulette shark
Hemiscyllium strahani – Hooded carpetshark
Hemiscyllium trispeculare – Speckled carpetshark

Family GINGLYMOSTOMATIDAE – Nurse Sharks
Ginglymostoma cirratum – Nurse shark
Nebrius ferrugineus – Tawny nurse shark or giant sleepy shark
Pseudoginglymostoma brevicaudatum – Shorttail nurse shark

Family STEGOSTOMATIDAE – Zebra Sharks
Stegostoma fasciatum – Zebra shark

Family RHINCODONTIDAE – Whale Sharks
Rhincodon typus – Whale shark

ORDER: LAMNIFORMES: Mackerel Sharks
Family ODONTASPIDIDAE – Sandtiger Sharks
Carcharias taurus – Sandtiger, spotted raggedtooth, or grey nurse shark
Odontaspis ferox – Smalltooth sandtiger or bumpytail raggedtooth
Odontaspis noronhai – Bigeye sandtiger

Family PSEUDOCARCHARIIDAE – Crocodile Sharks
Pseudocarcharias kamoharai – Crocodile shark

Family MITSUKURINIDAE – Goblin Sharks
Mitsukurina owstoni – Goblin shark

Family MEGACHASMIDAE – Megamouth Sharks
Megachasma pelagios – Megamouth Shark

Family ALOPIIDAE – Thresher Sharks
Alopias pelagicus – Pelagic thresher
Alopias superciliosus – Bigeye thresher
Alopias vulpinus – Thresher shark

Family CETORHINIDAE – Basking Sharks
Cetorhinus maximus – Basking shark

Family LAMNIDAE – Mackerel Sharks
Carcharodon carcharias – White shark
Isurus oxyrinchus – Shortfin mako
Isurus paucus – Longfin mako
Lamna ditropis – Salmon shark
Lamna nasus – Porbeagle shark

ORDER: CARCHARHINIFORMES: Ground Sharks
Family SCYLIORHINIDAE – Catsharks
Apristurus albisoma – White-bodied catshark
Apristurus aphyodes – White ghost catshark
Apristurus brunneus – Brown catshark
Apristurus canutus – Hoary catshark

Apristurus exsanguis – Flaccid catshark
Apristurus fedorovi – Stout catshark
Apristurus gibbosus – Humpback catshark
Apristurus herklotsi – Longfin catshark
Apristurus indicus – Smallbelly catshark
Apristrurus internatus – Shortnose demon catshark
Apristurus investigatoris – Broadnose catshark
Apristurus japonicus – Japanese catshark
Apristurus kampae – Longnose catshark
Apristurus laurussoni – Iceland catshark
Apristurus longicephalus – Longhead catshark
Apristurus macrorhynchus – Flathead catshark
Apristurus macrostomus – Broadmouth catshark
Apristurus manis – Ghost catshark
Apristurus microps – Smalleye catshark
Apristurus micropterygeus – Smalldorsal catshark
Apristurus nasutus – Largenose catshark
Apristurus parvipinnis – Smallfin catshark
Apristurus pinguis – Fat catshark
Apristurus platyrhynchus – Spatulasnout catshark
Apristurus profundorum – Deepwater catshark
Apristurus riveri – Broadgill catshark
Apristurus saldanha – Saldanha catshark
Apristurus sibogae – Pale catshark
Apristurus sinensis – South China catshark
Apristurus spongiceps – Spongehead catshark
Apristurus stenseni – Panama ghost catshark
Apristurus sp. A – Freckled catshark
Apristurus sp. B   Bigfin catshark
Apristurus sp. C – Fleshynose catshark
Apristurus sp. D – Roughskin catshark
Apristurus sp. E – Bulldog catshark
Apristurus sp. F – Bighead catshark
Apristurus sp. G – Pinocchio catshark
Asymbolus analis – Grey spotted catshark
Asymbolus funebris – Blotched catshark
Asymbolus occiduus – Western spotted catshark
Asymbolus pallidus – Pale spotted catshark
Asymbolus parvus – Dwarf catshark
Asymbolus rubiginosus – Orange spotted catshark
Asymbolus submaculatus – Variegated catshark
Asymbolus vincenti – Gulf catshark
Atelomycterus fasciatus – Banded sand catshark
Atelomycterus macleayi – Australian marbled catshark
Atelomycterus marmoratus – Coral catshark
Aulohalaelurus kanakorum – New Caledonia catshark
Aulohalaelurus labiosus – Blackspotted catshark
Bythaelurus canescens – Dusky catshark
Bythaelurus clevai – Broadhead catshark
Bythaelurus dawsoni – New Zealand catshark
Bythaelurus hispidus – Bristly catshark
Bythaelurus immaculatus – Spotless catshark
Bythaelurus lutarius – Mud catshark
Bythaelurus sp. B – Galapagos catshark
Cephaloscyllium fasciatum – Reticulated swellshark
Cephaloscyllium isabellum – Draughtsboard shark
Cephaloscyllium laticeps – Australian swellshark
Cephaloscyllium silasi – Indian swellshark
Cephaloscyllium sufflans – Balloon shark
Cephaloscyllium umbratile – Japanese swellshark
Cephaloscyllium ventriosum – Swellshark
Cephaloscyllium sp. A – Whitefin swellshark
Cephaloscyllium sp. B – Saddled swellshark
Cephaloscyllium sp. C – Northern draughtboard shark
Cephaloscyllium sp. D – Narrowbar swellshark
Cephaloscyllium sp. E – Speckled swellshark
Cephaloscyllium sp. F – Dwarf oriental swellshark
Cephalurus cephalus – Lollipop catshark
Cephalarus sp. A – Southern lollipop catshark
Galeus antillensis – Antilles catshark
Galeus arae – Roughtail catshark
Galeus atlanticus – Atlantic sawtail catshark
Galeus boardmani – Australian sawtail catshark
Galeus cadenati – Longfin sawtail catshark
Galeus eastmani – Gecko catshark
Galeus gracilis – Slender sawtail catshark
Galeus longirostrus – Longnose sawtail catshark
Galeus melastomus – Blackmouth catshark
Galeus mincaronei – Southern sawtail catshark
Galeus murinus – Mouse catshark
Galeus nipponensis – Broadfin sawtail catshark
Galeus piperatus – Peppered catshark
Galeus polli – African sawtail catshark
Galeus sauteri – Blacktip sawtail catshark
Galeus schultzi – Dwarf sawtail catshark
Galeus springeri – Springer's sawtail catshark
Galeus sp. B – Northern sawtail catshark
Halaelurus boesemani – Speckled catshark
Halaelurus buergeri – Darkspot/Blackspotted catshark

Halaelurus lineatus – Lined catshark
Halaelurus natalensis – Tiger catshark
Halaelurus quagga – Quagga catshark
Haploblepharus edwardsii – Puffadder shyshark or Happy Eddie
Haploblepharus fuscus – Brown shyshark or Plain Happy
Haploblepharus pictus – Dark shyshark or Pretty Happy
Holohalaelurus punctatus – Whitespotted or African spotted catshark
Holohalaelurus regani – Izak catshark
Holohalaelurus polystigma – East African spotted catshark or Grinning Izak
Parmaturus campechiensis – Campeche catshark
Parmaturus macmillani – New Zealand filetail
Parmaturus melanobranchius – Blackgill catshark
Parmaturus pilosus – Salamander shark
Parmaturus xaniurus – Filetail catshark
Parmaturus sp. A – Shorttail catshark
Pentanchus profundicolus – Onefin catshark
Poroderma africanum – Striped catshark or pajama shark
Poroderma pantherinum – Leopard catshark
Schroederichthys bivius – Narrowmouth catshark
Schroederichthys chilensis – Redspotted catshark
Schroederichthys maculatus – Narrowtail catshark
Schroederichthys saurisqualus – Southern sawtail
Schroederichthys tenuis – Slender catshark
Scyliorhinus besnardi – Polkadot catshark
Scyliorhinus boa – Boa catshark
Scyliorhinus canicula – Smallspotted catshark
Scyliorhinus capensis – Yellowspotted catshark
Scyliorhinus cervigoni – West African catshark
Scyliorhinus comoroensis – Comoro catshark
Scyliorhinus garmani – Brownspotted catshark
Scyliorhinus haeckelii – Freckled catshark
Scyliorhinus hesperius – Whitesaddled catshark
Scyliorhinus meadi – Blotched catshark
Scyliorhinus retifer – Chain catshark
Scyliorhinus stellaris – Nursehound
Scyliorhinus tokubee – Izu catshark
Scyliorhinus torazame – Cloudy catshark
Scyliorhinus torrei – Dwarf catshark

Family PROSCYLLIIDAE – Finback Catsharks
Ctenacis fehlmanni – Harlequin catshark
Eridacnis barbouri – Cuban ribbontail catshark
Eridacnis radcliffei – Pygmy ribbontail catshark
Eridacnis sinuans – African ribbontail catshark
Proscyllium habereri – Graceful catshark
Proscyllium sp. A – Clown or magnificent catshark

Family PSEUDOTRIAKIDAE – False Catsharks
Gollum attentuatus – Slender smoothhound
Gollum sp. A – Sulu gollumshark
Gollum sp. B – Whitemarked gollumshark
Pseudotriakis microdon – False catshark

Family LEPTOCHARIIDAE – Barbeled Houndshark
Leptocharias smithii – Barbeled houndshark

Family TRIAKIDAE – Houndsharks
Furgaleus macki – Whiskery shark
Galeorhinus galeus – Tope shark, soupfin shark, or school shark
Gogolia filewoodi – Sailback houndshark
Hemitriakis abdita – Darksnout or Deepwater sicklefin houndshark
Hemitriakis falcate – Sicklefin houndshark
Hemitriakis japanica – Japanese topeshark
Hemitriakis leucoperiptera – Whitefin topeshark
Hemitriakis sp. A – Ocellate topeshark
Hypogaleus hyugaensis – Blacktip topeshark or pencil shark
Iago garricki – Longnose houndshark
Iago omanensis – Bigeye houndshark
Mustelus antarcticus – Gummy shark
Mustelus asterias – Starry smoothhound
Mustelus californicus – Grey smoothhound
Mustelus canis – Dusky smoothhound
Mustelus dorsalis – Sharpnose smoothhound
Mustelus fasciatus – Striped smoothhound
Mustelus griseus – Spotless smoothhound
Mustelus henlei – Brown smoothhound
Mustelus higmani – Smalleye smoothhound
Mustelus lenticulatus – Spotted estuary smoothhound or rig
Mustelus lunulatus – Sicklefin smoothhound
Mustelus manazo – Starspotted smoothhound
Mustelus mento – Speckled smoothhound
Mustelus minicanis – Venezuelan dwarf smoothhound
Mustelus mosis – Arabian, hardnose, or Moses smoothhound
Mustelus mustelus – Smoothhound

Mustelus norrisi – Narrowfin or Florida smoothhound
Mustelus palumbes – Whitespot smoothhound
Mustelus punctulatus – Blackspot smoothhound
Mustelus schmitti – Narrownose smoothhound
Mustelus sinusmexicanus – Gulf of Mexico smoothhound
Mustelus whitneyi – Humpback smoothhound
Mustelus sp. A – Grey gummy shark
Mustelus sp. B – Whitespotted gummy shark
Scylliogaleus quecketti – Flapnose houndshark
Triakis acutipinna – Sharpfin houndshark
Triakis maculata – Spotted houndshark
Triakis megalopterus – Spotted gully shark
Triakis scyllium – Banded houndshark
Triakis semifasciata – Leopard shark

Family HEMIGALEIDAE – Weasel sharks
Chaenogaleus macrostoma – Hooktooth shark
Hemigaleus microstoma – Sicklefin weasel shark
Hemigaleus sp. A – Australian weasel shark
Hemipristis elongatus – Snaggletooth shark
Paragaleus leucolomatus – Whitetip weasel shark
Paragaleus pectoralis – Atlantic weasel shark
Paragaleus randalli – Slender weasel shark
Paragaleus tengi – Straighttooth weasel shark

Family CARCHARHINIDAE – Requiem sharks
Carcharhinus acronotus – Blacknose shark
Carcharhinus albimarginatus – Silvertip shark
Carcharhinus altimus – Bignose shark
Carcharhinus amblyrhynchoides – Graceful shark
Carcharhinus amblyrhynchos – Grey reef shark
Carcharhinus amboinensis – Pigeye or Java shark
Carcharhinus borneensis – Borneo shark
Carcharhinus brachyurus – Copper shark or bronze whaler
Carcharhinus brevipinna – Spinner shark
Carcharhinus cautus – Nervous shark
Carcharhinus dussumieri – Whitecheek shark
Carcharhinus falciformis – Silky shark
Carcharhinus fitzroyensis – Creek whaler
Carcharhinus galapagensis – Galapagos shark
Carcharhinus hemiodon – Pondicherry shark
Carcharhinus isodon – Finetooth shark
Carcharhinus leiodon – Smooththooth blacktip
Carcharhinus leucas – Bull or Zambezi shark
Carcharhinus limbatus – Blacktip shark
Carcharhinus longimanus – Oceanic whitetip shark
Carcharhinus macloti – Hardnose shark
Carcharhinus melanopterus – Blacktip reef shark
Carcharhinus obscurus – Dusky shark
Carcharhinus perezi – Caribbean reef shark
Carcharhinus plumbeus – Sandbar shark
Carcharhinus porosus – Smalltail shark
Carcharhinus sealei – Blackspot shark
Carcharhinus signatus – Night shark
Carcharhinus sorrah – Spottail shark
Carcharhinus tilsoni – Australian blacktip shark
Carcharhinus sp. A – False smalltail shark
Galeocerdo cuvier – Tiger shark
Glyphis gangeticus – Ganges shark
Glyphis glyphis – Speartooth shark
Glyphis siamensis – Irrawaddy River shark
Glyphis sp. B – Borneo River shark
Glyphis sp. C – New Guinea River shark
Isogomphodon oxyrhynchus – Daggernose shark
Lamiopsis temmincki – Broadfin shark
Loxodon macrorhinus – Sliteye shark
Nasolamia velox – Whitenose shark
Negaprion acutidens – Sharptooth lemon shark
Negaprion brevirostris – Lemon shark
Prionace glauca – Blue shark
Rhizoprionodon acutus – Milk shark
Rhizoprionodon lalandei – Brazilian sharpnose shark
Rhizoprionodon longurio – Pacific sharpnose shark
Rhizoprionodon oligolinx – Grey sharpnose shark
Rhizoprionodon porosus – Carribean sharpnose shark
Rhizoprionodon taylori – Australian sharpnose shark
Rhizoprionodon terraenovae – Atlantic sharpnose shark
Scoliodon laticaudus – Spadenose shark
Triaenodon obesus – Whitetip reef shark

Family SPHYRNIDAE – Hammerhead sharks
Eusphyra blochii – Winghead shark
Sphyrna corona – Mallethead shark
Sphyrna lewini – Scalloped hammerhead
Sphyrna media – Scoophead shark
Sphyrna mokarran – Great hammerhead
Sphyrna tiburo – Bonnethead shark
Sphyrna tudes – Smalleye hammerhead
Sphyrna zygaena – Smooth hammerhead

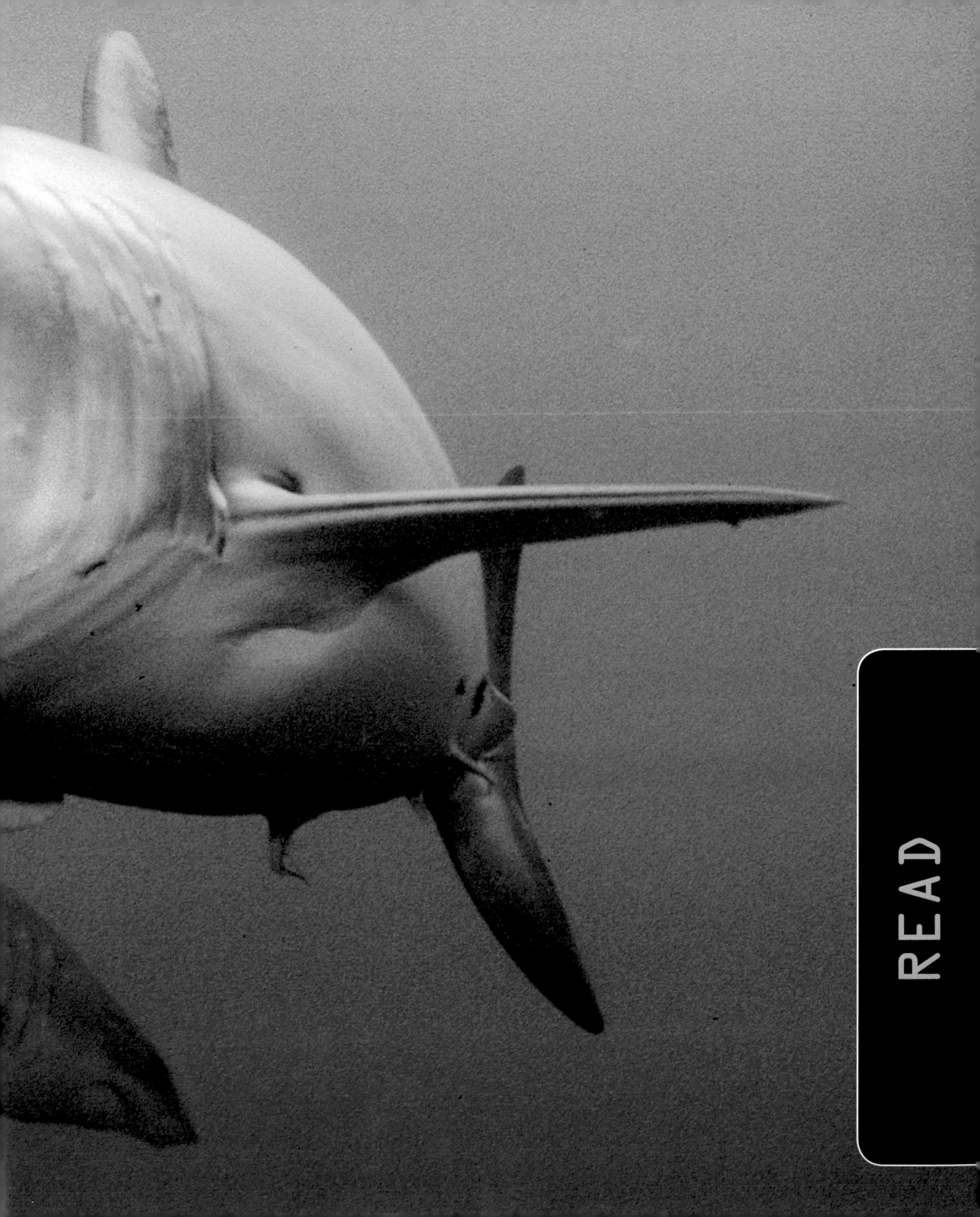

Introduction

Much of shark tracking has to do with waiting: waiting for the weather to clear, waiting for equipment to boot up, waiting for funding to come through, and waiting, waiting, waiting for sharks to arrive. So what keeps a tracker busy during all this waiting? Reading books and watching movies.

Most of the books and movies out there—from the classics to the modern—portray sharks as mindless, man-eating devils. And while we know that this is unfair and untrue, sometimes it makes for a good story!

Read on to meet 19th-century whalers fighting to keep sharks away from their mighty catch, and an old fisherman struggling to repel the sharks that threaten his prize—and his life. You'll even meet the toothy star of the most famous shark movie of all time: *Jaws*.

So dive in to these amazing sharky sagas. Some are gruesome, some are glorious, but all are fun.

EDITOR'S NOTE

There's no way we could fit all the works that feature sharks in here, so what follows is just a smattering of classic fiction. But you should know that there are chum buckets full of nonfiction essays, books, and documentaries that celebrate sharks and inform the world of the importance of these incredible marine predators.

The Old Man and the Sea

The *Old Man and the Sea* is perhaps Ernest Hemingway's most famous and widely read book. It debuted in 1952 to much acclaim, and earned Hemingway the Pulitzer Prize in 1953. While this story is mostly about an old fisherman's pursuit of a marlin, it is also about his respect for the sea and all the animals that live within it.

BIG FISH

A marlin is a type of large game fish that can reach lengths of more than 16 feet (5 m). It has a long body, an elongated, spearlike snout, and a rigid dorsal fin that rises off the body to form a crest.

SAVE THE BEST FOR LAST

The Old Man and the Sea was the last book Hemingway published before his death in 1961.

Hemingway with a marlin

ERNEST HEMINGWAY

Ernest Hemingway was one of the most famous and influential authors of the 20th century. He was born in Oak Park, Illinois, in 1899. After starting his career as a journalist in 1917, he volunteered as an ambulance driver in Italy during World War I, a time that greatly influenced his writing. He lived in Paris for much of the 1920s, where he wrote some of his most famous works. Later he lived in Key West, Florida, and Cuba. In addition to the Pulitzer, Hemingway won the 1954 Nobel Prize for Literature. He took his own life in 1961.

Selected Bibliography:

The Sun Also Rises 1926
A Farewell to Arms 1929
For Whom the Bell Tolls 1940
The Old Man and the Sea 1952
A Moveable Feast (published posthumously) 1964

Santiago is an old Cuban fisherman who, after 84 days of bad fishing, lands a mighty marlin. The giant fish is no easy catch, however, and over two days and nights, the marlin and Santiago battle. Though Santiago grows to respect and admire the fish, he is glad when it finally weakens. He lashes it to his skiff (a small boat) and, exhausted, turns toward home. Then the hungry sharks come and ravage his glorious catch.

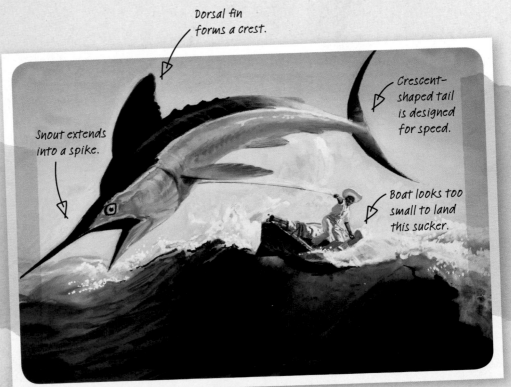

Dorsal fin forms a crest.

Crescent-shaped tail is designed for speed.

Snout extends into a spike.

Boat looks too small to land this sucker.

AFTER BATTLING THE MARLIN for two days and nights, Santiago has finally killed the fish and lashed it to his boat. He is exhausted and in pain, and hopes that his sail home will be clear and easy. He should be so lucky . . .

They sailed well and the old man soaked his hands in the salt water and tried to keep his head clear. There were high cumulus clouds and enough cirrus above them so that the old man knew the breeze would last all night. The old man looked at the fish constantly to make sure it was true. It was an hour before the first shark hit him.

The shark was not an accident. He had come up from deep down in the water as the dark cloud of blood had settled and dispersed in the mile deep sea. He had come up so fast and absolutely without caution that he broke the surface of the blue water and was in the sun. Then he fell back into the sea and picked up the scent and started swimming on the course the skiff and the fish had taken.

Sometimes he lost the scent. But he would pick it up again, or have just a trace of it, and he swam fast and hard on the course. He was a very big Mako shark, built to swim as fast as the fastest fish in the sea and everything about him was beautiful except his jaws. His back was as blue as a sword fish's and his belly was silver and his hide was smooth and handsome. He was built as a swordfish except for his huge jaws. Which were tight shut now as he swam fast, just under the surface with his high dorsal fin knifing through the water without wavering. Inside the closed double lip of his jaws all of his eight rows of teeth were slanted inwards. They were not the ordinary pyramid-shaped teeth of most sharks. They were shaped like a man's fingers when they are crisped like claws. They were nearly as long as the fingers of the old man and they had razor-sharp cutting edges on both sides. This was a fish built to feed on all the fishes in the sea, that were so fast and strong and well armed that they had no other enemy. Now he speeded up as he smelled the fresher scent and his blue dorsal fin cut the water.

When the old man saw him coming he knew that this was a shark that had no fear at all and would do exactly what he wished. He prepared the harpoon and made the rope fast while he watched the shark come on. The rope was short as it lacked what he had cut away to lash the fish.

The old man's head was clear and good now and he was full of resolution, but he had little hope. It was too good to last, he thought. He took one look at the great fish as he watched the shark close in. It might as well have been a dream, he thought. I cannot keep him from hitting me but maybe I can get him. *Dentuso*, he thought. Bad luck to your mother.

The shark closed fast astern and when he hit the fish the old man saw his mouth open and his strange eyes and the clicking chop of the teeth as he drove forward in the meat just above the tail. The shark's head was out of the water and his back was coming out and the old man could hear the noise of skin and flesh ripping on the big fish when he rammed the harpoon down onto the shark's head at a spot where the line between his eyes intersected with the line that ran straight back from his nose. There were no such lines. There was only the heavy sharp blue head and the big eyes and the clicking, thrusting all-swallowing jaws. But that was the location of the brain and the old man hit it. He hit it with his blood-mushed hands driving a good harpoon with all his strength. He hit it without hope but with resolution and complete malignancy.

The shark swung over and the old

man saw his eye was not alive and then he swung over once again, wrapping himself in two loops of the rope. The old man knew that he was dead but the shark would not accept it. Then, on his back, with his tail lashing and his jaws clicking, the shark plowed over the water as a speed-boat does. The water was white where his tail beat it and three-quarters of his body was clear above the water when the rope came taut, shivered, and then snapped. The shark lay quietly for a little while on the surface and the old man watched him. Then he went down very slowly.

"He took about forty pounds," the old man said aloud. He took my harpoon too and all the rope, he thought, and now my fish bleeds again and there will be others.

He did not like to look at the fish anymore since he had been mutilated. When the fish had been hit it was as though he himself were hit.

But I killed the shark that hit my fish, he thought. And he was the biggest *dentuso* that I have ever seen. And God knows that I have seen big ones.

It was too good to last, he thought. I wish it had been a dream now and that I had never hooked the fish and was alone in bed on the newspapers.

"But man is not made for defeat," he said. "A man can be destroyed but not defeated." I am sorry that I killed the fish though. Now the bad time is coming and I do not even have the harpoon. The *dentuso* is cruel and able and strong and intelligent. But I was more intelligent than he was. Perhaps not, he thought. Perhaps I was only better armed.

"Don't think, old man," he said aloud. "Sail on this course and take it when it comes."

But I must think, he thought. Because it is all I have left. That and baseball. I wonder how the great DiMaggio would have liked the way I hit him in the brain? It was no great thing, he thought. Any man could do it. But do you think my hands were as great a handicap as the bone spurs? I cannot know. I never had anything wrong with my heel except the time the stingray stung it when I stepped on him when swimming and paralyzed the lower leg and made the unbearable pain.

"Think about something cheerful, old man," he said. "Every minute now you are closer to home. You sail lighter for the loss of forty pounds."

He knew quite well the pattern of what could happen when he reached the inner part of the current. But there was nothing to be done now.

"Yes there is," he said aloud. "I can lash my knife to the butt of one of the oars."

So he did that with the tiller under his arm and the sheet of the sail under his foot.

"Now," he said. "I am still an old man. But I am not unarmed."

The breeze was fresh now and he sailed on well. He watched only the forward part of the fish and some of his hope returned.

It is silly not to hope, he thought. Besides I believe it is a sin. Do not think about sin, he thought. There are enough problems now without sin. Also I have no understanding of it.

I have no understanding of it and I am not sure that I believe in it. Perhaps it was a sin to kill the fish. I suppose it was even though I did it to keep me alive and feed many people. But then everything is a sin. Do not think about sin. It is much too late for that and there are people who are paid to do it. Let them think about it. You were born to be a fisherman as the fish was born to be a fish. San Pedro was a fisherman as was the father of the great DiMaggio.

But he liked to think about all things that he was involved in and since there was nothing to read and he did not have a radio, he thought much and he kept on thinking about sin. You did not kill the fish only to keep alive and to sell for food, he thought. You killed him for pride and because you are a fisherman.

You loved him when he was alive and you loved him after. If you love him, it is not a sin to kill him. Or is it more?

"You think too much, old man," he said aloud.

But you enjoyed killing the *dentuso*, he thought. He lives on the live fish as you do. He is not a scavenger nor just a moving appetite as some sharks are. He is beautiful and noble and knows no fear of anything.

"I killed him in self-defense," the old man said aloud. "And I killed him well."

Besides, he thought, everything kills everything else in some way. Fishing kills me exactly as it keeps me alive. The boy keeps me alive, he thought. I must not deceive myself too much.

He leaned over the side and pulled loose a piece of the meat of the fish where the shark had cut him. He chewed it and noted its quality and its good taste. It was firm and juicy, like meat, but it was not red. There was no stringiness in it and he knew that it would bring the highest price in the market. But there was no way to keep its scent out of the water and the old man knew that a very bad time was coming.

The breeze was steady. It had backed a little further into the north-east and he knew that meant that it would not fall off. The old man looked ahead of him but he could see no sails nor could he see the hull nor the smoke of any ship. There were only the dying fish that went up from his bow sailing away to either side and the yellow patches of Gulf weed. He could not even see a bird.

He had sailed for two hours, resting in the stern and sometimes chewing a bit of the meat from the marlin, trying to rest and to be strong, when he saw the first of the two sharks.

"Ay," he said aloud. There is no translation for this word and perhaps it is just a noise such as a man might make, involuntarily, feeling the nail go through his hands and into the wood.

"*Galanos,*" he said aloud. He had seen the second fin now coming up behind the first and had identified them as shovel-nosed sharks by the brown, triangular fin and the sweeping movements of the tail. They had the scent and were excited and in the stupidity of their great hunger they were losing and finding the scent in their excitement. But they were closing all the time.

The old man made the sheet fast and jammed the tiller. Then he took up the oar with the knife lashed to it. He lifted it as lightly as he could because his hands rebelled at the pain. Then he opened and closed them on it lightly to loosen them. He closed them firmly so they would take the pain now and would not flinch and watched the sharks come. He could see their wide, flattened shovel-pointed heads now and their white-tipped wide pectoral fins. They were hateful sharks, bad smelling, scavengers as well as killers, and when they were hungry they would bite at an oar or the rudder of a boat. It was these sharks that would cut the turtles' legs and dippers when the turtles were asleep on the surface, and they would hit a man in the water, if they were hungry, even if the man had no smell of fish blood nor of fish slime on him.

"Ay," the old man said. "*Galanos* Come on, *galanos*"

They came. But they did not come as the Mako had come. One turned and went out of sight under the skiff and the old man could feel the skiff shake as he jerked and pulled on the fish. The other watched the old man with his slitted yellow eyes and then came in fast with his half circle of jaws wide to hit the fish where he had already been bitten. The line showed clearly on the top of his brown head and back where the brain joined the spinal cord and the old man drove the knife on the oar into the juncture, withdrew it, and drove it in again into the shark's yellow cat-like eyes. The shark let go of the fish and slid down, swallowing what he had taken as he died.

The skiff was still shaking with the destruction the other shark was doing to the fish and the old man let go the sheet so that the skiff would swing broadside and bring the shark out from under. When he saw the shark he leaned over the side and punched at him. He hit only meat and the hide was set hard and he barely got the knife in. The blow hurt not only his hands but his shoulder too. But the shark came up fast with his head out and the old man hit him squarely in the center of his flat-topped head as his nose came out of the water and lay against the fish. The old man withdrew the blade and punched the shark exactly in the same spot again. He still hung to the fish with his jaws hooked and the old man stabbed him in his left eye. The shark still hung there.

"No?" the old man said and he drove the blade between the vertebrae and the brain. It was an easy shot now and he felt the cartilage sever. The old man reversed the oar and put the blade between the shark's jaws to open them. He twisted the blade and as the shark slid loose he said, "Go on, *galano*. Slide down a mile deep. Go see your friend, or maybe it's your mother."

The old man wiped the blade of his knife and laid down the oar. Then he found the sheet and the sail filled and be brought the skiff onto her course.

Moby Dick

Yes, *Moby Dick* is about whales, not sharks. But it's about so much more than that! This dark tale of obsession takes the reader on a whirlwind adventure 'cross the Seven Seas. Sure, there be whales in these waters, but there be sharks, too.

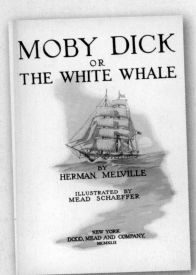

← *An old title page*

SLOW START

Published in 1851, *Moby Dick* did not get very good reviews. In fact, it was deemed a failure during Melville's lifetime. Today, however, it is considered one of the greatest novels in the English language. Its opening line, "Call me Ishmael," is one of the most famous in the world.

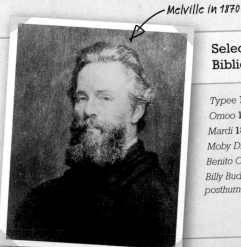

Melville in 1870

HERMAN MELVILLE

Herman Melville was born in 1819. His father died when Melville was 13, leaving the family with almost nothing. As an adult, Melville joined the crew of a whaler, an experience that had a great impact on him. His first novels, *Typee* and *Omoo*, were each a huge success. And while he wrote until his death in 1891, none of his other work garnered as much attention as these first two novels. *Moby Dick* wasn't a hit until the 20th century.

Selected Bibliography:

Typee **1846**
Omoo **1847**
Mardi **1849**
Moby Dick **1851**
Benito Cereno **1855**
Billy Budd, Sailor (published posthumously) **1924**

Main characters	**Ishmael**, narrator, sailor on the *Pequod* **Queequeg**, harpooner, and friend of Ishmael	**Ahab**, obsessed, crazy captain of the *Pequod* **Stubb**, second mate

Ishmael is looking for adventure, and enlists as an oarsman on the whaler *Pequod*. The other men on the ship seem to be hardworking, and all starts off swimmingly. The peg-legged Captain Ahab, however, is moody and erratic. While at sea, he reveals that his only goal for this voyage is to find and kill Moby Dick, the great white whale that bit off his leg. In fact, he cares about nothing else in the world. This blind obsession leads the *Pequod* and its crew on a dark and doomed journey across the globe.

Lashing a whale to a ship was no easy task.

HAVING CAUGHT A WHALE and lashed it to the side of the ship, the crew of the *Pequod* prepares for a long night of fending off the sharks that are attracted to the blood in the water. As was common on whaling ships, they used sharp blades attached to long, wooden poles to slash and stab at sharks. I warn you, Melville wasn't really a conservationist. The following excerpt comes off as a bit cruel, and more-than-a-bit gross.

chapter 66

THE SHARK MASSACRE

When in the Southern Fishery a captured Sperm Whale, after long and weary toil, is brought alongside late at night, it is not, as a general thing at least, customary to proceed at once to the business of cutting him in. For that business is an exceedingly laborious one; is not very soon completed; and requires all hands to set about it. Therefore, the common usage is to take in all sail; lash the helm a'lee; and then send every one below to his hammock till daylight, with the reservation that, until that time, anchor-watches shall be kept; that is, two and two for an hour, each couple, the crew in rotation shall mount the deck to see that all goes well.

But sometimes, especially upon the Line in the Pacific, this plan will not answer at all; because such incalculable hosts of sharks gather round the moored carcase, that were he left so for six hours, say, on a stretch, little more than the skeleton would be visible by morning. In most other parts of the ocean, however, where these fish do not so largely abound, their wondrous voracity can be at times considerably diminished, by vigorously stirring them up with sharp whaling-spades, a procedure notwithstanding, which, in some instances, only seems to tickle them into still greater activity. But it was not thus in the present case with the *Pequod*'s sharks; though, to be sure, any man unaccustomed to such sights, to have looked over her side that night, would have almost thought the whole round sea was one huge cheese, and those sharks the maggots in it.

Nevertheless, upon Stubb setting the anchor-watch after his supper was concluded; and when, accordingly Queequeg and a forecastle seaman came on deck, no small excitement was created among the sharks; for immediately suspending the cutting stages over the side, and lowering three lanterns, so that they cast long gleams of light over the turbid sea, these two mariners, darting their long whaling-spades,* kept up an incessant murdering of the sharks, by striking the keen steel deep into their skulls, seemingly their only vital part. But in the foamy confusion of their mixed and struggling hosts, the marksmen could not always hit their mark; and this brought about new revelations of the incredible ferocity of the foe. They viciously snapped, not only at each other's disembowelments, but like flexible bows, bent round, and bit their own; till those entrails seemed swallowed over and over again by the same mouth, to be oppositely voided by the gaping wound. Nor was this all. It was unsafe to meddle with the corpses and ghosts of these creatures. A sort of generic or Pantheistic vitality seemed to lurk in their very joints and bones, after what might be called the individual life

had departed. Killed and hoisted on deck for the sake of his skin, one of these sharks almost took poor Queequeg's hand off, when he tried to shut down the dead lid of his murderous jaw.

*The whaling-spade used for cutting-in is made of the very best steel; is about the bigness of a man's spread hand; and in general shape, corresponds to the garden implement after which it is named; only its sides are perfectly flat, and its upper end considerably narrower than the lower. This weapon is always kept as sharp as possible; and when being used is occasionally honed, just like a razor. In its socket, a stiff pole, from twenty to thirty feet long, is inserted for a handle.

"Queequeg no care what god made him shark," said the savage, agonizingly lifting his hand up and down; "wedder Fejee god or Nantucket god; but de god wat made shark must be one dam Ingin."

The Narrative of Arthur Gordon Pym

Even Edgar Allan Poe—master of the dark, creepy tale—got in on the shark action! As in many stories, the sharks in this one play a supporting role, but their presence reinforces the sense of doom that hangs over Pym and his companion as they sail ever farther from home.

MIXED REVIEWS

Many feel that this is one of Poe's stranger tales. Some scholars think its structure and style were ahead of its time, and many find rich religious meaning and symbolism in its pages. Others think it's just weird and boring. The reviewers in Poe's time were split, too: The book had a small following, especially in England, but most readers passed it over. (Poe himself called it "a very silly book.")

Poe was famous for his dark, macabre stories.

EDGAR ALLAN POE

Edgar Poe was born on January 19, 1809, in Boston. After the death of his parents, young Edgar moved in with the Allan family of Richmond, Virginia. He moved again—to Baltimore, Philadelphia, and New York—as he pursued a writing career. Poe was unique in his day for earning a living only through writing, though this led to financial difficulty. In 1845, he published his famous poem, "The Raven." He died in 1849, at the age of 40.

Selected Bibliography:

The Narrative of Arthur Gordon Pym 1838
The Fall of the House of Usher 1839
The Tell-Tale Heart 1843
The Raven 1845
The Cask of Amontillado 1846

Arthur Pym, thirsty for adventure, stows away with his friend Augustus Barnard on a whaling ship. After a mutiny and a terrible storm, the survivors resort to cannibalism to stay alive. Sadly, Barnard dies, and is cast overboard to the sharks. Pym faces ever more dark and mysterious threats right up to the strange ending. What becomes of Pym? Perhaps only the sharks know. . . .

HARD TIMES

Two installments of *Pym* were first published in Richmond's *Southern Literary Messenger* in 1837, when Poe was an editor there. However, before the whole story could be told, he was fired. He moved to New York to find writing work, but it was very hard to come by. Poe lived in poverty as he revised his first novel for publication.

THE NARRATIVE

OF

ARTHUR GORDON PYM.

OF NANTUCKET.

COMPRISING THE DETAILS OF A MUTINY AND ATROCIOUS BUTCHERY ON BOARD THE AMERICAN BRIG GRAMPUS, ON HER WAY TO THE SOUTH SEAS, IN THE MONTH OF JUNE, 1827.

WITH AN ACCOUNT OF THE RECAPTURE OF THE VESSEL BY THE SURVIVERS; THEIR SHIPWRECK AND SUBSEQUENT HORRIBLE SUFFERINGS FROM FAMINE; THEIR DELIVERANCE BY MEANS OF THE BRITISH SCHOONER JANE GUY; THE BRIEF CRUISE OF THIS LATTER VESSEL IN THE ANTARCTIC OCEAN; HER CAPTURE, AND THE MASSACRE OF HER CREW AMONG A GROUP OF ISLANDS IN THE

EIGHTY-FOURTH PARALLEL OF SOUTHERN LATITUDE;

TOGETHER WITH THE INCREDIBLE ADVENTURES AND DISCOVERIES

STILL FARTHER SOUTH

TO WHICH THAT DISTRESSING CALAMITY GAVE RISE.

NEW-YORK:

HARPER & BROTHERS, 82 CLIFF-ST.

1838.

The first complete edition was published in 1838 under this descriptive bookplate.

Jaws

The 1975 film *Jaws* is a terrifying tale of a man-eating shark that targets a beach town. It was a huge success nationwide, and catapulted its actors and young director into stardom. Unfortunately, it also demonized sharks the world over. Opening June 20, 1975, the movie eventually grossed more than $470 million (today that would be more than $1.8 *billion*), and is considered the first summer blockbuster.

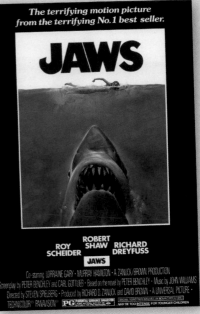

1975 movie poster

INSPIRATION

Jaws is based on the 1974 novel written by Peter Benchley.

Twenty-nine-year old director

STEVEN SPIELBERG

Steven Spielberg was born in Cincinnati, Ohio, on December 18, 1946. In his early teens, he started making short films that featured his sisters and the Arizona desert where he spent much of his childhood. *Jaws* was Spielberg's second major film. Its enormous success catapulted the 29-year-old director to stardom, and earned him the right to creative freedom on his subsequent movies. He has become one of Hollywood's most famous and influential directors.

Selected Filmography:

Jaws 1975
Raiders of the Lost Ark 1981
E.T.: the Extra-Terrestrial 1982
Jurassic Park 1993
Schindler's List 1993
Indiana Jones and the Kingdom of the Crystal Skull 2008

It's summertime, the crowds have flocked to Amity Island for another season, and the town's new police chief, Martin Brody, is getting acquainted with the mayor, the tourists, and the locals.

When the body of a young shark-attack victim washes ashore, Brody quietly calls in biologist Matt Hooper. When the shark strikes again—in front of a beach full of terrified people—the town hires a grizzled local shark-hunter named Quint.

Soon, the three men embark on a gut-wrenching journey into the Atlantic to silence the menace. Not all of them return.

Will Brody make it, or will the shark prevail?

Index

A

ampullae of Lorenzini 16, 23, 63
anatomy
  of rays 16
  of sharks 18–19, 21, 34, 45
angel shark 20, 38, 42
art 85
Atlantic weasel shark 35
attacks
  blue shark 58
  bull shark 75, 78, 94
  carpetshark 54
  causes 94, 95
  how to avoid 96–97
  map 98–99
  number per year 94
  oceanic whitetip shark 56, 61
  tiger shark 61, 83
  USS *Indianapolis* 61
  white shark 89, 94

B

baby sharks 18, 19, 23, 55, 63
balance, sense of 23
barbels 22, 28, 38, 41, 50, 51, 52
barbelthroat shark 50
basking shark 45, 46–47, 49
bearded wobbegong. *See* tasselled
  wobbegong
Benchley, Peter. See *Jaws* (novel)
bigeye thresher 64, 101
bioluminescence 26, 31, 34
birth 19, 42, 55, 80
bite, strongest 101
blacktip reef shark 22, 56
blacktip shark 57
blind shark 54
blood circulation 18, 68
blue shark 58, 61, 101
bluntnose sixgill 33
bonnethead shark 66
bouyancy 18, 71
bramble shark 39, 101
breaching 65, 69, 88, 91
breathing and respiration 18, 19, 51
Briggs, Capt. Thomas 13
brownbanded bambooshark 51
brown-spotted catshark. *See* brownbanded
  bambooshark
bulldog shark 79. *See also* Port Jackson shark
bullhead sharks 20, 41
bull shark 57, 74–77, 78–79, 95, 99

C

camera, underwater 9

cannibalism 19, 27, 59, 69, 76
captivity, sharks in 42, 48, 55, 66, 85, 90
capture. *See* captivity, sharks in; fishing
  for shark
Carcharodon megalodon 15
carpetsharks 20, 50–53, 54
cartilage 18, 47
catsharks 21, 28–29, 31, 35, 51
chain catshark 28
chimaera 16, 17
cold- and warm-bodied sharks 18, 69
commercial uses
  cartilage 47
  fins 35, 47, 49, 65, 83
  liver oil 27, 33, 47, 65
  meat 27, 37, 47
  medicinal substances 18, 30, 55
  skin 27, 47, 65
  spines 41
conservation 37, 42, 47, 49, 83
cookiecutter shark 31, 34
cooking with shark 35, 37, 49, 65, 83
copper shark 37
Cousteau, Jacques-Yves 9
cow sharks 32, 33
"crawling" on the ocean bottom 38, 53
crocodile shark 33

D E

denticles. *See* skin, dermal denticles
depth, extreme 33, 39, 40, 46, 87, 101
digestion 19, 82
distance traveled 91, 101
diving 46, 48
dogfish sharks 20, 26–27, 28, 30, 39–40
dusky shark 37, 101
dwarf lanternshark 100

ears and hearing 23
eggs 19, 29
electroreception 16, 23, 63
elephant fish 17
endangered species 38, 51, 67, 70, 73. *See
  also* threatened and vulnerable species
epaulette shark 21, 50, 51
eyes and vision 21, 62, 87, 101

F G

fastest shark 101
feelers. *See* barbels
fiction, classic. *See Moby Dick; The Narrative
  of Arthur Gordon Pym; The Old Man and
  the Sea*
filter feeders 44–47
fins
  "crawling" on the ocean bottom 38, 53
  function 19

notches on 91
shark fin soup 35, 49, 65, 83
fishing for shark 12, 47, 65, 68
flotation strategies 18, 71
folklore and myths 12–13, 47, 51
food chain 36, 37
food of rays 16
food of sharks
  cannibalism 19, 27, 59, 69, 76
  digestion 19, 82
  fat-rich 88
  plankton 44–47
  scavenged or dead 40, 77, 82, 84
  shark bait 9, 89
  time between meals 19
fossils 15, 36
Fox, Rodney 95
frilled shark 39, 43, 100

genetics 66
gestation 76, 100
gill raker 45, 46
gills 19, 46
glowing. *See* bioluminescence
goblin shark 40
gray nurse shark. *See* sandtiger shark
great hammerhead shark 63
great white shark. *See* white shark
Greenland shark 40
grey bambooshark 100
guitarfish 16, 17

H I J

Hamilton, Bethany 95
hammerhead sharks 20, 21, 62–63, 67, 96
hearing. *See* ears and hearing
Hemingway, Ernest 10. See also *The Old Man
  and the Sea*
Hirst, Damien 85
holocephalan 16
home range 38
horn shark 21. *See also* Port Jackson shark
houndsharks 35
Hybodus 15, 17

Ichthyosaurus 14
identification of sharks 20, 44, 91
intelligence 85

Jaws (movie) 88, 94, 120–121
Jaws (novel) 88, 120
jumping. *See* breaching

L M N

lantern sharks 26, 31
largest shark 100
lateral line 21, 39

Resources

Learn more about sharks, research, and conservation at these Web sites:

SHARK RESEARCH INSTITUTE
www.sharks.org

THE SHARK TRUST
www.sharktrust.org

INTERNATIONAL SHARK ATTACK FILE
www.flmnh.ufl.edu/fish/Sharks/ISAF/ISAF.htm
(keeps records of all reported shark attacks worldwide since the year 1580)

REEFQUEST CENTRE FOR SHARK RESEARCH
www.elasmo-research.org

Photo Credits

DK would like to thank the following photographers for their contributions to this project. Every effort has been made to trace copyright holders. DK Publishing apologizes for any unintentional omissions, and would be pleased, if any such case should arise, to add an appropriate acknowledgment in future editions.

Acknowledgments

Many, many shark trackers gave their time and energy to make this book, and they all deserve a whale-shark-sized thanks.

Very special thanks go to Marie Levine and Erich Ritter at the Shark Research Institute for their time and expertise.

SHARK RESEARCH INSTITUTE (SRI) is an international scientific organization that conducts and sponsors research on sharks, and promotes their conservation. Programs include tracking worldwide migrations of sharks using satellite and radio telemetry, ocean advocacy, visual ID catalogues, DNA studies, population and behavioral studies, publications, and public education. SRI also maintains the Global Shark Attack File for medical professionals and the media who need accurate information about shark/human interactions. SRI researchers are working in the United States, the Bahamas, Canada, China, Costa Rica, Ecuador, Honduras, India, Mexico, Mozambique, Seychelles, South Africa, Taiwan, and Tanzania. Learn more at **www.sharks.org**

NANCY ELLWOOD would like to thank Beth Hester, Alisha Niehaus, John Searcy, Kate Ritchey, Niki Foreman, and Nanette Cardon for their input and hard work. Jessica Park for her artistic vision and stamina. Michelle Baxter and Beth Sutinis for their guidance. Nancy P. Ellwood for her constant support. Michael J. Fasulo for his unfailing enthusiasm, humor, and interest in the sharks of the world.

MARGARET PARRISH would like to say thanks to Geert, Sarah, and Belia for spending several months hearing about all things shark.

JESSICA PARK would like to thank Diana Catherines, Mark J. Davies, and Susan St. Louis for helping with design. Chrissy McIntyre for finding such beautiful images. Katherine Yam and her team at Colourscan for color reproduction.